HONEY
FROM
STONE

A Naturalist's Search for God

CHET RAYMO

Illustrations by Bob O'Cathail

Dodd, Mead & Company, Inc.   •   New York

First Edition

10 9 8 7 6 5 4 3 2 1

Library of Congress Cataloging-in-Publication Data

Raymo, Chet.
    Honey from stone.

        1. Religion and science—1946–   —Meditations.
2. Nature—Religious aspects—Meditations.   I. Title.
BL240.2.R35   1987   215   87-19053
ISBN 0-396-08996-8

Book design and production by Eric Newman

For Maurice Sheehy,
friend and guide
to the Dingle Peninsula.

CONTENTS

INTRODUCTION

Three hundred million years ago the rocks of Ireland were gently squeezed from the south. The rocks were caused to fold, accordion-wise, in northeast/southwest–tending pleats. The rocks that folded upward became mountains, and the rocks that folded downward became valleys. Time passed, and the level of the sea rose with respect to the land. The valleys were flooded.

Today, those ancient pleats in Ireland's crust form a series of peninsulas that reach into the Atlantic like the fingers of a hand. The northernmost finger is the Dingle Peninsula. It is a place of misty mountains and green fields, towering sea-cliffs and beaches of yellow sand. It is a quiet place, reached by two roads that hang precariously between the mountains and the sea. The peninsula has been mostly bypassed by industrial civilization, and unreliable weather keeps away the hordes of tourists who would otherwise be drawn by the region's breathtaking beauty. For eight years I have made my summer home on the peninsula. For twice that long I have been a regular visitor.

The Dingle Peninsula is rich in the relics of human habitation. It has more antiquities per square mile than almost any other place in Europe. From the pre-Christian era there are ring forts, promontory forts, souterranes, recumbent megaliths, and alignments of standing stones. Many of these have associations with the myths and legends of Irish prehistory. From Christian times there are stone crosses, ogham stones (stones marked with an early Irish alphabet), and some of the most remarkable unmortared stone architecture in all of the world. It is impossible to move among these mysterious relics without feeling something of the hold of history. History leaves its imprint upon a physical landscape; it also leaves an indelible impression upon the landscapes of our souls.

I was raised in a traditional religion that made much of "indelible signs," but early on I abandoned the theology and religious practices of my youth. I took academic degrees in science, and I found in science a compelling vision of reality. I do not mean to say that I turned science into a religion; science is too shallow a vessel to hold ultimate mysteries. Rather, in science I discovered a universe of wonderful dimension, complexity, and beauty. It was a universe that folded inward to embrace the helical dance of the DNA, and outward to enclose the enigmatic quasars and spiraling galaxies. In the face of such a universe, the narrowly anthropomorphic forms of traditional theology seemed inadequate. Nothing of what I had been taught in my religious education seemed quite capacious enough to encompass what I learned in science.

But the hold of history—personal and cultural—is not easily shaken off. After several decades during which

I held to the secure ground of science, an attraction to the circumscribing ambient of mystery continued to make itself felt. Perhaps it was something of the physical and spiritual geography of the Dingle Peninsula that caused me to reinitiate the religious quest. The questions I now asked were these: What is the relevance of traditional religion in the world described by contemporary science? Is scientific knowledge a satisfactory ground for the religious experience? Can the language of traditional religion constitute an appropriately modern language of praise?

The meditations that follow are an attempt to answer these questions. They are loosely framed as a Book of Hours. In the medieval monastic tradition the day was divided into eight canonical "hours"—Matins, Lauds, Prime, Terce, Sext, Nones, Vespers, and Compline—each with assigned observances. A Book of Hours was a collection of meditations or prayers to be read or recited at the appropriate time of day. These essays follow that convention. Each of them grew out of an experience that occurred at approximately the canonical hour. Although I have written the book in the present tense, it should be clear that the experiences I describe did not occur on the same day or even in the same year. The title—*Honey from Stone*—is borrowed from a passage of Saint Bernard of Clairvaux that stands as the epigraph for the book. The title has a literal as well as a metaphorical connotation. No feature of the landscape of the Dingle Peninsula is more prevalent than stone. When I had completed these meditations, I realized that stone figures prominently in each of them.

This is not a work of metaphysics or theology. It is instead a kind of serendipitous adventure, a spiritual vagabond's quest. I have tramped the landscapes of the

Dingle Peninsula, studying the rocks, the sky, the flora and the fauna, and I took whatever scraps of revelation I could find. I sought the burning bush and did not find it. But I found the honeysuckle and the fuchsia, and I found the gorse and the heather. When I called out for the Absolute, I was answered by the wind. If it was God's voice in the wind, then I heard it.

ACKNOWLEDGMENTS

Warm thanks to Robert Goulet, Bartley MacPháidín, and Maureen Raymo for making important contributions to the book. The Naughtons, the Holsteads, and the Sheehys of Ventry, Ireland, were companions and friends as the book was written. Mary Kennan, friend and editor at Dodd, Mead, exerted throughout a sustaining influence on my work. Bob O'Cathail's linocuts make the book a thing of beauty. Eric Newman helped polish the manuscript. Especially, I thank Maurice Sheehy for sharing with me over the course of a dozen years his considerable knowledge of the Dingle Peninsula.

LAUDS: My version of The Song of Amergin draws on several published translations, including those of Douglas Hyde and Thomas Kinsella, and the assistance of Maurice Sheehy. TERCE: Ralph R. Horne's *Geological Guide to the Dingle Peninsula*, Geological Survey of Ireland, 1976, was an invaluable source. SEXT: Des Lavelle's *Skellig: Island Outpost of Europe*, The O'Brien Press, Dublin, 1976, was my guide to the islands. NONES: Two works of great help for this meditation were Martin J.S. Rudwick, *The Great Devonian Controversy: The Shaping of Scientific Knowledge Among Gentlemen*

Specialists, University of Chicago Press, Chicago, 1985; and Gordon L. Herries Davies, *Sheets of Many Colors: The Mapping of Ireland's Rocks 1750–1890*, Royal Dublin Society, Dublin, 1983. The latter was the source of the sketch portrait of Flanagan. VESPERS: I have drawn heavily upon that wonderful classic of Irish natural history, Robert Lloyd Praeger's *The Way That I Went*, Allen Figgis, Dublin, 1980. COMPLINE: The translations from the poetry of Saint John of the Cross are excerpted from John Frederick Nims, *The Poems of John of the Cross*, University of Chicago Press, Chicago, 1959, and are used with permission. Sources that were of general use throughout the book were Anne Bancroft, *The Luminous Vision: Six Medieval Mystics and Their Teachings*, George Allen & Unwin, London, 1982, and Robert Burnham Jr., *Burnham's Celestial Handbook*, Dover, 1978.

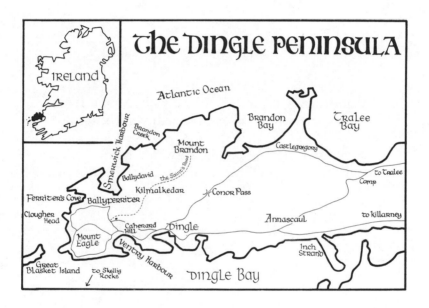

More things are learnt in the woods than from books; trees and rocks will teach you things not to be heard elsewhere. You will see for yourselves that honey may be gathered from stones and oil from the hardest rock....

St. Bernard of Clairvaux

MATINS

Put on Your Jumping Shoes

IF IT IS GOOD LUCK to see a falling star, then this is my lucky night. During an hour's walk along the dark high road from Dingle, in the west of Ireland, I have seen three dozen meteors, including one fireball so bright its light persisted from the zenith to the horizon. Meteors have been falling from the sky like foil confetti, unrolling like tinsel streamers. So many "stars" have fallen from the dome of night it is a wonder there are any left to define the constellations.

Tonight is the peak of the Perseid meteor shower of August, generally considered to be the strongest meteor shower of the year. Astronomy handbooks cite typical counts of twenty or thirty meteors per hour when the Perseids are at maximum. You are unlikely to see that many unless you have eyes like a fish that can take in a full 360 degrees of sky at once. But I have seen more than the predicted number, which means that tonight's shower is stronger than usual. Something's going on up there. Something's raising the count.

Meteor showers are associated with the trajectories of comets. As comets travel along their orbits, they shed a part of their substance. A comet's tail is made of matter blown away from the comet by sunlight. Eventually the tracks of comets become dirty spaces, littered with material discarded by the comet in its passage—icy grit, bits of stone—moving more or less in the same orbit as the comet but spread out before the comet and behind it like harbingers and train. Every year in August the Earth intersects the orbit of Comet Swift-Tuttle. As the Earth moves across the comet's track it sweeps up cometary debris. These particles plunge into the Earth's atmosphere, where they are heated by friction and vaporized. It is the tracks of burning vapor that we see as "shooting stars" or "falling stars"—not stars at all, but grains of cosmic dust making spectacular swan dives into the Earth's atmosphere. It has been estimated that there are one hundred million tons of particulate matter spread out along the orbit of Comet Swift-Tuttle; tonight I have seen a few ounces' worth of that matter streak across the sky.

And where is the comet itself, Comet Swift-Tuttle, the parent of this prodigious stream? It was last near the orbit of the Earth in 1862. In that year Comet Swift-Tuttle was a spectacular naked-eye object, with a nucleus, a coma, and a tail. According to all reports, it was one of the finest comets of the century. From calculations based on observations made at that time, astronomers anticipated the return of Comet Swift-Tuttle in 1984, after a century-long journey far out beyond the planet Pluto. The time of the expected arrival is past, and still there is no sign of the returning comet. Perhaps tonight's brilliant harvest of meteors is an intimation that the comet is coming near.

The orbit of Comet Swift-Tuttle is steeply inclined to the orbit of the Earth. It dives down out of the northern sky, crosses the Earth's own trajectory, and then swings away to the south. Tonight's meteors approach along that same path. The place in the sky where a meteor shower seems to originate is called the radiant of the shower; the radiant of the shower of mid-August is in the constellation Perseus, and the meteors are called Perseids. The shooting stars I see tonight appear in every part of the sky, from horizon to horizon, but the lines of their motion, if traced backward, intersect, like the lines of a perspective drawing, in the starless space between Perseus and Cassiopeia, high in the northeastern sky. The streaks of meteoric light are like the spokes of a wheel that has its rim in the constellations of the horizon—Taurus, Ursa Major, Hercules, Aquarius—and its hub in Perseus. When Comet Swift-Tuttle comes—*if* it comes—it will approach along the axle of that wheel.

An old moon rose tonight at midnight with the winter stars of Taurus. It is still low on the southern horizon, its sleepy eye half closed. Summer nights are short at the latitude of Ireland, and already in the northern sky there is a trace of rosy light that anticipates the dawn. It is morning. It is the morning of the Feast of Saint Lawrence.

In many rural parts of Europe the Perseid meteors are called the Tears of Saint Lawrence. I have known the story of Lawrence since I was a child. It is the kind of story that was certain to make an impression upon a young mind. Even now, forty years later, I remember its first telling: how Decius, upon becoming emperor of the Roman Empire, began a persecution of Christians. For

Lawrence he devised a special torture. He prepared a sort of barbecue grill that he placed above a fire of glowing coals. He stripped Lawrence and pressed him upon the grill to roast. "Turn me over," said the saint after an appropriate interval of torment. "I'm done on this side."

The story of the martyrdom of Lawrence, like much hagiography of early saints, is almost certainly apocryphal. There is little primary historical evidence that would verify the saint's existence. The characters in the story, as I heard it, did not even live at the same time. Still, when I heard the story as a child, I regarded it as fact. Lawrence was presented to me as a real-life actor in the drama of faith and salvation. "Whom should I adore," asked the saint accusingly, when the emperor demanded worship of the ancient gods, "the Creator or the creature?" It was a huge question. And in reply, Decius had Lawrence whipped with scorpions.

What am I to make of the story now, forty years later? Lawrence's story is a child's story. But the question asked by the saint echoes across the years: *Whom should I adore, the Creator or the creature?* And what is the answer? The creation is here, palpably present, on this night of shooting stars. The sky weeps meteors. The Milky Way stands like a pillar on the sea. And where is the Creator, the God of Lawrence? Gone. Flown away on some heavenward trajectory, like Comet Swift-Tuttle, into the darkness at the edge of knowing.

Decius was a general in the army of Philip, the first Christian emperor. Philip sent Decius to subdue an uprising of the Gauls, which was readily accomplished. The general returned to Rome in triumph and, as was often the case with successful and ambitious generals, usurped the power of empire. The victorious commander ordered Philip killed. And to cover the murder and his own vaulting ambition, he cloaked the act as a righteous move to return the empire to the worship of the ancient gods. At that time, Sixtus was the pope of Rome and Lawrence was his deacon. Decius arrested Sixtus and arranged his execution, but not before the pope had a chance to direct his deacon to distribute the congregation's treasure to the poor. Decius heard rumors of silver candlesticks and chalices of gold. He had Lawrence brought before him and demanded the treasure. Lawrence asked for three days to get the treasure in order. On the third day, he gathered before Decius the poor, the weak, and the infirm of Rome. *"This* is the Church's treasure," said Lawrence. The emperor was not pleased. "You will pass this night in torment," he said to the saint. And then Lawrence spoke the words that ring like a bell through the prayers of his feast: "Night has no darkness for me, but all things become visible in the light."

Tonight, in the west of Ireland, the sky is streaked with light. Meteors flash like fireworks. The fuchsias in the hedgerows are soaked with starlight; the honeysuckle glistens. In the east, the moon closes its milky white eye; in the west, the Milky Way sinks into the sea. My thoughts are with the Psalmist: "When I behold the heavens, the work of your fingers, the moon and the stars

which you set in place, what is man that you should be mindful of him?" And I have no answer. I am alone. In all of this heavenly light I am alone and the night is dark.

The night is dark! The night is huge and fearful and wonderfully dark. The stars are hot coals glowing in the darkness—I roast in their heat. What falls from the sky are not a saint's tears. What falls from the sky are bits and pieces of a scattered comet. And there's another one hundred million tons of the stuff yet to fall.

◗

The Perseid meteors are swift. They streak into the Earth's atmosphere at 40 miles per second, 150 thousand miles per hour. They sizzle in the air. They are swift because the Earth encounters the stream of cometary particles head on, like an automobile driving into the rain, rather than being overtaken from behind. During the course of a single night the Earth will fly half a million miles across the stream of the Perseids, sweeping up billions of them. The planet will add tons to its bulk— tons of sky dust plastered onto the planet like raindrops on a windshield. Some of the dust will survive its dive through the atmosphere and settle onto the planet's surface. Scientists can dig down into Arctic or Antarctic ice and collect Perseids that fell to Earth a thousand years ago. They can collect Perseids that fell to Earth during the night Saint Lawrence spent on the grill.

If a meteor glows more brightly than the planet Venus, it is called a fireball. The fireball I saw tonight was bright enough to be reflected in the sea. It entered the atmosphere high overhead and fell toward the horizon out across Dingle Bay. It met its image streaking across

the water. Pliny the Elder, the Roman natural philosopher, described stones that fell from the sky, and
chunks of iron that resembled sponges. He also recorded a
rain of milk and blood, and a rain of flesh. Once, he tells
us, wool fell from the sky, and on another occasion it
rained baked bricks. So, what is all this material that is
skittering about in the night? Is the universe full of wool
and blood and baked bricks on huge galactic trajectories?
Tonight the Earth hurtles along its circular orbit for half a
million miles toward the star Aldebaran. Meanwhile, the
sun, and the Earth with it, flies like a shot toward Vega.
The galaxy whirls on its axis; during the few seconds the
fireball was in the air, the turning galaxy carried me a
hundred miles. And the galaxies are not fixed; they
scatter like shrapnel from the impulse of the Big Bang.
On the scale of the galaxy, the Earth is a grain of dust,
flying on its orbit like a Perseid. On the scale of the
universe, the galaxy is a drop of milk or blood. The whole
affair is like one of those miniature atomic explosions the
physicist watches in a cloud chamber—scintillations,
radiations, alphas and betas, particles making tracks,
matter skittering, apparently random, without purpose.

From the place where I watched the fireball fall into
the sea, the road rises to a cleft in the ridge above Ventry
village, to a place called Maumanorig, "the pass of the
springs." Here I meet the hedgehog. It comes scuttling
toward me out of the ditch, a small, tottering shadow, and
it stops dead just at my feet. I know at once what it is,
even in the light of a closing moon—this bristly shadow,
this clump of ditch and bramble that has flung itself into
the road. I snap on my flashlight and get down upon my
knees. The hedgehog, sensing my attention, curls up into

a ball. It is the size of my closed fist; it looks more like a
sea urchin than a mammal. I examine it in my light. I
have picked up hedgehogs in my hand—it is an operation
that must be done with care—but this one I just tip over,
using my flashlight as a prod. It rolls onto its spines, as
rigid as a cradle, the moist snout snugly pressed against
the fleshy belly. The soft pads of the paws are as bright as
opals. The hedgehog's feeble eyes are closed; perhaps it is
afraid of what might be seen, or playing dead. But I am
the one who is afraid of what might be seen if those eyes
open, those eyes accustomed to the darkness of the ditch
and the starless night of the burrow. The hedgehog
quivers with fear, and I know that if the eyes open they
will be overbrimming with terror, spilling over with an
inarticulate prayer. There will be no cocky certainty for
the hedgehog, no asking to be roasted on the other side.
The hedgehog lives all of its life in a crown of thorns. I
read somewhere that if you pester a hedgehog too much
or for too long it will die as its only means of escape.

This creature would fit into the cup of my hands, if it
weren't for the prickles. A female hedgehog, when she
mates, will flatten her spines against her fur so that the
male can mount her without damage to his soft under-
belly. A hedgehog is designed soft side down, spikes to
the stars. It is armored against everything but the soil;

how would a fox get a purchase on this macelike fist? I flick off my light; the hedgehog doesn't move. I walk a dozen paces along the road, downwind, and wait; still no motion. I move farther on, until I can barely make out the dark form of the animal, and I wait again—five minutes, then ten. The hedgehog remains fixed—fixed by fear, fixed by the huge intrusion of my light.

◑

Comets take their names from their discoverers. Comet Swift-Tuttle, the parent comet of the Perseids, was first observed by Lewis Swift, a farmer of Marathon, New York, and Horace Tuttle of the Harvard College Observatory.

To call Lewis Swift a farmer is not quite accurate. The farm was his livelihood, but his passion was the sky. On every clear night Swift observed the heavens with a 4¼" refractor telescope mounted on a platform attached to his barn. The discovery that changed his life was made on the evening of July 15, 1862. On that night Swift observed a blur of light in the dark, starless sky of the constellation Camelopardalis, just to the north and east of Perseus. The blur was bright—an object of the eighth magnitude—bright enough to place it within easy reach of binoculars. The object had the appearance of a comet, but Swift thought it unlikely that a comet could have reached this magnitude of brightness without having been previously noticed by someone else. He reluctantly concluded that what he had seen was the recently discovered Comet Schmidt. Three nights later Horace Tuttle, in Cambridge, Massachusetts, observed the same blur in Camelopardalis and immediately recognized its significance. It was, in fact, the fifth comet that Tuttle had discovered. On that same evening, Lewis Swift realized his error and reported the new object. According to protocol, the two men shared the honor of discovery. The comet is known as Swift-Tuttle, 1862 III.

The comet quickly brightened to become a splendid naked-eye object. The French astronomer Camille Flammarion called it one of the ten finest comets of the century. During July and August, as the armies of the Union and the Confederacy moved toward the decisive slaughter at Antietam Creek, Comet Swift-Tuttle drew closer to the sun and blossomed in reflected sunlight. Nineteenth-century drawings of the comet have been reproduced in the NASA *Atlas of Cometary Forms* (the drawings were made by J. F. Julius Schmidt of the Athens Observatory and P. A. Secchi of the Observatory of the Collegio Romano); they show fountains of light erupting from the nucleus of the comet and arcs of sun-blown particles, sowing the trajectory with the meteoric matter of future showers.

Comet Swift-Tuttle passed perihelion, its closest approach to the sun, on August 23, 1862, and then quickly receded into the southern sky. It was last observed from the Cape Observatory in South Africa on October 27. But that was not the end of Comet Swift-Tuttle. In 1867, the Italian astronomer Giovanni Schiaparelli announced that the calculated orbit of the comet of 1862 was coincident with the orbit of the Perseid meteors of August. This was compelling evidence that the Perseid meteors are material that has somehow become detached from the comet, perhaps on earlier orbits of the comet around the sun. It was the first time that a recurring shower of meteors was convincingly related to the orbit of a periodic comet.

Lewis Swift went on to discover a total of thirteen comets, although none equaled in brightness the comet of 1862. For his work with comets he was awarded a gold medal by the Imperial Academy of Sciences in Vienna. In the 1880s he was appointed to the directorship of the Warner Observatory in Rochester, New York, and from the people of that city he received a 16-inch refractor telescope costing $11,000. With that instrument the ex-farmer discovered more than a thousand nebulas.

From Maumanorig the road dips down along an inflection in the slope of the hill. It is now little more than a track—two tracks, really, of lime and crushed stone with a grassy median. To my right, rough pasturage climbs steeply through heather and furze to where it meets the stars of the Great Bear, half-hidden behind the brow of the hill; to my left, fields of closely nibbled grass fall away toward the sea. The road is bounded on both sides by hedgerows of bramble and fuschia that are twice as high as a man. Except where the hedgerows are broken by a gate, my attention is directed upward, to the open mouth of that cornucopia in Perseus that is pouring out stone. Somewhere up there in the throat of that spacy horn is Comet Swift-Tuttle, long approaching and now overdue.

Comets presumably have their origin in the so-called Oort cloud, named for the Dutch astronomer who proposed its existence, a spherical halo of cold, dark matter in cometlike clumps that surrounds our solar system and reaches out halfway to the nearest stars. Many astronomers believe that the Oort cloud consists of frozen leftovers from the formation of the solar system. There is perhaps enough matter in the Oort cloud for a million billion comets, stashed in the deep freeze of interstellar space. Now and then a passing star will gravitationally disturb the cloud and send a comet or a swarm of comets streaming into the inner part of our solar system. If one of these comets passes close to a large planet and gets a gravitational "kick," it can be forced into a periodic orbit that will keep it close to the sun. Comet Swift-Tuttle is such a comet; if it was born in the Oort cloud, it now finds itself bound to a track that does not take it much farther from the sun than the orbit of Pluto.

Comets are the roller coasters of the solar system. At the "top" of their cigar-shaped orbits they glide with exceeding slowness through the dusky outer reaches of the solar system. As they turn to fall toward the sun, they gather speed. Faster and faster they fall, down across the orbits of the planets. At last they whip around the sun with neck-snapping velocity and begin their slow climb back up to the top of the track. Comet Swift-Tuttle was at the top of its track at about the time I was born, in 1936. Throughout my life—now half a century—it has been falling toward the sun, tumbling like a boulder down a hill, accelerating. But where is it? Are the calculations of the astronomers wrong? Was the orbit perturbed from the calculated trajectory when the comet passed near some unknown body, "up there" at the top of the track? Has the comet been blown away by the solar wind, dispersed into these zillion bits and pieces that fall from the zenith even as I walk? Could I gather up the remains of Comet Swift-Tuttle in a bushel basket?

As meteor showers go, the Perseids are reliable. A graph of the frequency of their occurrence (meteor counts per hour) repeats itself almost exactly from year to year. I could very nearly tell you the day of the year by counting shooting stars. But the shower's parent comet may not be so exactly predictable. And this is why: The nucleus of a comet has been likened to a dirty snowball. It consists of dusts and ices. As a comet passes near to the sun, the sun's heat causes the ices on the sunlit side of the nucleus to sublime (pass directly from the solid to the gaseous state). Molecules of gas shoot outward from the comet at speeds of several hundred feet per second, toward the sun and in a direction perpendicular to the comet's motion. This "jet effect" pushes the comet away from the sun but doesn't change the comet's speed or the shape of the orbit. However, if the comet's nucleus is rotating—and every celestial object has *some* spin—then the subliming molecules will be thrown toward the back or the front of the moving comet, depending on the direction of spin. Now the "jet effect" will either speed the comet up or slow it down. The shape of the orbit will be changed. The comet will return earlier or later than a simple gravitational calculation would indicate. This makes the prediction of the time for the return of a comet an uncertain business. So the astronomers may be wrong. I won't give up yet on Comet Swift-Tuttle. I will keep watching that patch of sky between Polaris and Perseus where the comet will appear—if it appears at all. The best possible outcome would be for the comet to arrive at the orbit of the Earth in August, on the Feast of Saint Lawrence, when the Earth is at the place where the orbit of the comet and the orbit of the Earth almost intersect. That close encounter would provide a spectacular show—not just the tears of Saint Lawrence, but the saint himself, the parent comet, tumbling out of darkness, suffused in a night-dispelling halo of light.

I stop at an especially dark spot in the road and look into Perseus. Even without optical aid I can make out the faint figure-eight blur of light that is the famous Double Cluster of Perseus, two clusters of hundreds of stars 8,000 light-years away. But no comet. I am not surprised. If the comet is there, then someone must have seen it before now. There are hundreds of comet hunters in the world, amateurs and professionals, present-day Swifts and Tuttles who hope to be the first to see the returning comet. Every night they look into the dark sky north of Perseus with the biggest and best optical instruments money can buy. There is a kind of glory to be had in the discovery of a comet—or in the recovery of a comet that has visited before. There are people who do nothing else but search for blurry lights in the night sky. When Comet Swift-Tuttle returns, one of those people will be the first to see it. So I do not see Comet Swift-Tuttle, but during the time I stand looking up into Perseus I count two or three more of the Tears of Saint Lawrence streaking earthward along the comet's path.

On the 22nd day of June 1633, Galileo Galilei, age sixty-nine, knelt before the assembled Congregation of the Holy Office in the convent of Santa Maria Sopra Minerva in Rome and read, haltingly, what had been written out for him. He forswore his belief that it is the sun, and not the Earth, that is the center of the universe. He forswore his conviction that the Earth moved. He renounced his own life's work as false and heretical. Legend has it that when the formal recantation had been spoken, Galileo touched the ground and murmured *"E pur si muove"*—"and yet it moves." It is unlikely that the story of Galileo's whispered remark is true, but it is equally unlikely that anyone in the assembled congregation, and certainly not the old scientist himself, took the recantation seriously. What the Church demanded was not so much assent to the doctrine of the immobility of the Earth as a public affirmation of the Church's authority. The irony of the episode is that Galileo's forced recantation did nothing to slow the advance of science. Issac Newton was born in the year of Galileo's death, and the Age of Reason was born with him. As a consequence of the Galileo affair, the Church cut itself off from participation in one of the great adventures of the human spirit—the flight of the human imagination with the soaring Earth into a universe of unanticipated majesty and mystery. By forgoing the adventure of science, the Church lost the opportunity of informing that new enterprise with the light of the mystical tradition. In going their separate ways, the Church and science were each impoverished: The Church remained committed to narrowly anthropomorphic theologies of the past, and science was deprived of access to the Church's rich traditional language of praise.

"The eye by which I see God is the same eye by which he sees me," said the fourteenth-century mystic Meister Eckhart. "My eye and the eye of God are one eye, one vision, one knowledge, and one love." Tonight I stand in a dark country lane in the west of Ireland and ride the

Earth on its skyrocket flight through space. Spinning like a top, the Earth carries me at a thousand miles per hour toward the constellation Orion, now rising in the east. The orbital motion of the Earth about the sun whisks me along at 68,000 miles per hour toward Aldebaran in Taurus. The motion of the sun among the stars of the galaxy adds 34,000 miles per hour to my velocity, and the turning of the Milky Way another 80,000 miles per hour. How do I manage to hang on for that terrifying ride? Why am I not blown tumbling backward, with sticks and branches from the hedgerows, with hedgehogs and badgers—a wind of creatures streaming in the Creator's wind, streaming like Perseids? Yes, the Earth moves. That blind old man on his knees in the convent of Santa Maria Sopra Minerva knew that the Earth moves, knew it against all the evidence of his senses and the opinion of the assembled churchmen. He saw it move with his mind's eye. He felt the force of the terrible wind. He held on for dear life and hoped that the force of that wind would blow his tormentors away.

In the winter of 1609, when Galileo turned his new telescope on the moon, he was the first to observe lunar craters. He did not call them craters; he referred to the circular depressions as "spots." Later in the century, Robert Hooke examined the lunar craters with a telescope and pointed out their similarity to certain volcanic features on Earth. He suggested two possible explanations for the craters on the moon: Bubbles of gas had burst through the lunar surface from within the body of the moon, or projectiles from the sky had punctured the surface. To test the latter theory, Hooke bombarded a mixture of pipe clay and water with a heavy body ("as a bullet") and produced round depressions not unlike those on the moon. But Hooke could not imagine "whence those bodies should come" that had apparently so pummeled the moon. Meteorites had not yet been admitted into the province of science.

Hooke had certainly heard stories of rocks that fell from the sky. Such stories had been circulating since antiquity (remember Pliny and the baked bricks!), but the stories were dismissed as superstition by the savants of the Scientific Revolution. In the eighteenth century, the prestigious Academy of Sciences at Paris attempted to put an end to the nonsense once and for all by decreeing that objects could *not* fall from the sky, whereupon European museums tossed out valuable collections of authentic meteorites. In America, when two Yale professors described a meteorite that fell in Connecticut, Thomas Jefferson is said to have remarked, "It is easier to believe that Yankee professors would lie than that stones would fall from heaven."

An infinite universe will always have the capacity to surprise. The Earth moves. And stones fall from heaven. Tonight, Perseids clatter to the Earth like hailstones. They embed themselves in Arctic ice caps. They sprinkle the forests of the Amazon with a fine cometary dust. Meteors clatter at my feet and I dance in the road. "Up, noble soul!" cried Meister Eckhart. "Put on your jumping shoes which are intellect and love." I put on my jumping shoes and go leaping between the hedgerows.

◗

Where the road drops down from Maumanorig to the castle at Rahinnane it is known as the *Bothar a caoine*, literally "the road of the head" (of the fields). A few of the older people in the village call it "the road of

the fairies." They say they have heard the wailing sound
of fairies on the hill at night. I have heard the "fairies" on
many a stormy night when the wind was from the north.
There is something about the way the wind becomes
turbulent where the slope of the hill abruptly changes
that sets up a spooky sing-song resonance. Some of my
neighbors are reluctant to walk the road at night; the hold
of traditional knowledge is strong, and even when reason
says "there are no fairies," something in the heart asserts
an older "truth." It is unfortunate that anyone would
eschew the high road at night, for it is a place of
exceptional beauty. The parish sleeps below, hugged by
hills and blanketed with green pastures. When the moon
is in the sky, the sea shimmers in concentric radiances—
Ventry Harbor, Dingle Bay, the Atlantic. On clear nights
there is a wonderful transparency to the air; I have seen
the star Antares, the "heart" of the Scorpion, standing so
close to the southern horizon that it appeared to touch
the sea. That transparency served me well tonight when I
saw a chunk of Comet Swift-Tuttle fall—or so it
seemed—sizzling into the dark Atlantic.

It has been estimated that every year the Earth
gathers up 100,000 tons of meteoric material from space.
Most of this material burns up in its passage through the
upper atmosphere, but five or six times each year someone witnesses the fall to the surface of a meteorite of
substantial size. The year 1969 was a particularly fruitful
year for meteorites. On February 8 a large shower of
stones fell near Allende, Mexico. More than two tons of
material of a very rare type was quickly gathered up and
passed on to scientists. On September 28 a second dramatic fall of stone occurred near Murchison, Australia,

and more than 500 kilograms of stone were collected. The Allende and Murchison meteorites revolutionized our understanding of the universe. Each of the falls held secrets of our beginnings.

The sun and planets came into existence nearly five billion years ago when a cloud of interstellar dust and gas collapsed under the influence of gravity to form a family of condensed spherical objects. The meteoric stones that fell on Mexico are thought to be survivors from those earliest days of the solar system. In the Allende stones there are white inclusions that contain chemical evidence for the kinds of nuclear reactions that are thought to occur only in the intensely energetic environments of exploding stars. The meteorite inclusions suggest that an exploding star—a supernova—may have been the trigger that caused our solar system to form. The shock wave from the supernova could have gathered up the gas and dust of interstellar space, like a push-broom sweeping dust before it. Then gravity would have clumped the gas and dust together to make a star and planets. If the clues in the Allende meteorite have been properly interpreted, the explosive death of an aging star was the stimulus that caused our own star, the sun, to be born.

The first undisputed discovery of amino acids of an extraterrestrial origin were found in the Murchison meteorites from Australia. Amino acids are the organic building blocks of the proteins. They are the chemical substrate for all life on Earth. If these organic compounds are common in meteoric material that comes from space, then life may be more prevalent in the universe than we once supposed. It is even possible that the first living organisms arrived on Earth as passengers on rocks from the sky. The Murchison meteorites hold out the hint that our microbial ancestors might literally have fallen out of the night.

The discoveries of supernova debris and amino acids within the materials of the Allende and Murchison meteorites affirm our unity with the rest of the universe. It is as Galileo guessed. The Earth, he said, "must not be excluded from the dancing whirl of stars." Meteorites have been found in the burial sites of North American Indians; the stones were probably considered by the Indians to be messengers from the gods and were placed in the graves so that they might accompany the souls of the dead back to heaven. The Indians were right. Stones that fall from the sky *are* messengers from heaven: In the mix of their elements they tell the story of our beginnings.

◗

Comet Swift-Tuttle has not arrived on schedule. Maybe we missed it altogether. Maybe it slipped by in February when the Earth was all the way around on the other side of its orbit. Maybe this night of shooting stars is all of Comet Swift-Tuttle I am going to get.

My house stands near the foot of "the road of the fairies," not far from where that track joins the main road to Ballyferriter. When I arrive at the house I do not go immediately to bed—there is very little of the night remaining—instead, I stretch out in a canvas chair in the front garden and continue to collect Perseids. "Show me the treasure!" commanded Decius, as Lawrence lay roasting on his bed of fire. And, here, I offer it—a scattering of diamonds, a moon like a silver chalice, a sky brocaded with constellations. "Whom should I adore," asked Lawrence, "the Creator or the creature?" And I am struck dumb; the question has no meaning. My eye and the eye of God are one eye—one vision, one knowledge, one love.

Lewis Swift, farmer and astronomer, fractured his hip at the age of thirteen and walked all his life with a limp. That disability did not prevent him from pursuing his great passion: "One can discover comets lying in bed," he said. He discovered thirteen comets and a thousand nebulas. Among those nebulas were hundreds of distant galaxies, star systems as extensive as the Milky Way, with trillions of suns, possibly teeming with planets and life. The prayer of Saint Lawrence might also have been the prayer of Lewis Swift: *Night has no darkness for me, but all things become visible in the light.* Lewis Swift's earliest and most famous discovery was the comet that is the progenitor of the Tears of Saint Lawrence. That shower of lights has illuminated this night. Tears continue to fall as dawn gathers in the east.

LAUDS

The God That Makes Fire in the Head

THE DAWN HAS BEEN ADVANCING for an hour, gathering in the hills behind Dingle, overbrimming the highest ridges and filling the valleys on the flanks of Brandon Mountain with tentative light. I have come to the megalithic tomb on the crest of Caherard Hill to await the sunrise. It is a single-chambered gallery grave, perhaps 5,000 years old. The walls of the tomb are flat slabs of sandstone, set vertically. Other slabs lie across the uprights to form the roof. Each of the stones weighs half a ton. They were dragged to the top of the hill from the cliffs along Ventry Harbour and set up to form a chamber twice as long and half as wide as a man is tall. A neolithic chieftain was laid to rest in the chamber with his funerary goods, and the entrance was sealed with another stone. Then the grave was heaped over with earth. The earth has been carried away by wind and time, but curb stones still define the perimeter of the original earthen mound. The tomb is known locally as the Giant's Bed (*leaba an fhir mhuimhnig*, "the bed of the Munsterman," it is called in Irish). I climb onto the tomb and stretch out on the horizontal capstones as if to sleep, carefully placing my body along the axis of the grave, and I watch the place on the horizon that is aligned between my feet as if in the sights of a gun. The grave is oriented to the east and west cardinal points of the compass. I have every expectation that when the sun rises, it will appear squarely between my toes.

It is the morning of the vernal equinox, one of two days each year when the sun rises exactly in the east and sets exactly in the west. It is the day when the sun moves back into the northern hemisphere of the sky and stands momentarily on the sky's equator. If I lived on the Earth's equator, at noon today the sun would pass directly above my head; here, at the latitude of Ireland (fifty-one degrees north), the sun will angle up on a sidling sort of path that will take it out above Dingle Bay and not much more than a third of the way up the sky from the southern horizon.

It is the fulcrum of the year, the balance point of the seasonal seesaw—winter is behind and summer is ahead. The people who built the gallery grave on Caherard Hill understood fulcrums; almost certainly they used levers to lift and move these huge slabs of stone. They understood balance; or how else could these stones have stood erect against the elements for 5,000 years? And they understood the sky and the way the sun moves rhythmically back and forth, north to south, south to north, like a bright gold amulet swung from a chain, measuring out the seasons, setting nature's beat. On Caherard Hill they laid a chieftain to rest in such a way that for all eternity his soul would be quickened by the light of the sun on that cardinal day in the spring when the sun moves back into northern skies and the seesaw tips toward fertility and green.

When Saint Patrick arrived in Ireland, it was with the worship of the sun that he contended in the name of the True God. He threatened the followers of the solar religion with hell fire. The sun, he preached, is not divine; it rises each day at *God's* bidding. At God's bidding? The sun comes up, that much is incontestable. On this first day of spring it will leap into expectant air— and at precisely the same point on the horizon where it has risen for 5,000 years.

◑

The sun was born out of an interstellar nebula of gas and dust. The nebula was many light-years wide, vastly larger than our present solar system. The material of the nebula was highly rarefied—a trillion times less dense than the Earth's atmosphere—but still much more concentrated than a typical part of the interstellar medium. The cloud was mostly hydrogen, with a generous sprinkling of helium. Other elements were there in traces; oxygen, neon, carbon, nitrogen, silicon, and iron were the most abundant. There were molecules of all sorts, including organic molecules such as those of alcohol, formaldehyde, and acetylene. There was carbon monoxide and ammonia. There was molecular water. And there were tiny grains of dust, as small as the point of a pin. The dust grains had cores of iron, sand, or graphite, and mantles of ice. All of the constitutents of the presolar cloud other than the hydrogen and helium amounted to no more than one percent of the cloud's mass.

Where did the materials in the presolar nebula come from? Were they there from the Beginning, from that instantaneous Creation the astronomers call the Big Bang? In the Beginning there was only light. At the first instant of time there was only a blinding flash of pure energy. As the universe expanded and cooled, the energy condensed into the primordial matter—protons, neutrons, and electrons. With more expansion and cooling, these particles bound themselves together into atoms of hydrogen and helium, but not yet into atoms of the heavier elements. Of the primordial hydrogen and helium, gravity formed stars and galaxies—refulgent galaxies, glittering stars. The stars proclaimed the glory of Creation, but there was as yet no solidity in the universe, no place where you could set your foot, no rock, no grit, no stem, no bone.

Deep in the hot cores of the stars, nature was patiently building, binding the nuclei of hydrogen and helium into heavier elements by a process called thermonuclear fusion. The stars built the heavy elements from the light ones, and the fusion released the energy that made the stars shine. Every starbeam that lit the early universe had its origin in the making of heavy elements. And when the stars were old and depleted and their nuclear fires flickered out, they had cores of carbon, silicon, oxygen, and iron. And some of the stars, the large ones, in their dying blew themselves apart and scattered their substance to space, so that slowly, as generations of stars lived and died, the universe's hoard of heavy elements increased.

The nebula that gave birth to our solar system had its share of the scattered stardust, a minute leavening of the heavy elements fused in stars. And as the nebula began to contract, what followed was the result of a delicate interplay of gravity and heat—gravity condensing, heat dispersing. The greater part of the substance of the nebula was pulled by gravity into a central sphere that became the sun. But the nebula had some degree of rotational motion, and as it contracted it spun faster and faster, as an ice skater spins faster when he pulls his arms closer to his body. The spinning cloud flattened out, like spinning pizza dough, into a whirling disk of gas and dust with a central spherical hub.

In the whirling disk, the heavier elements were collected by gravity into grains, and the grains into nuggets, and the nuggets into stones and clumps of iron. These knots of ponderous matter were still embedded in a much greater mass of hydrogen and helium and light volatile compounds. And then something remarkable happened: At the core of the contracting central sphere, the temperature reached ten million degrees. Fusion began. The central mass ignited as a new star, ignited with a terrible initial violence that astronomers call the T-Tauri stage of stellar evolution. A hurricane of energy blew outward from the new star and swept the inner part of the solar system clear of the lighter gases and compounds, except for those that were trapped inside the clumps of rock and iron. When enough time had passed, the clumps of rock and iron, now orbiting in empty space, were collected by gravity and mutual collisions into several large solid objects. One of them was Earth.

Of the gas and dust that were spread out over a billion billion cubic miles of the original nebula, only a few tiny bits—the heaviest bits, the ash of earlier stars—were gathered up into the planet Earth. The Earth was a mote of dust orbiting a central sun. That mote of dust and a few others like it are all that is left of the great cloud of material that surrounded the new sun just before it ignited as a star. The blast of radiation from the new star was like a broom that swept the solar system clean of light volatile gases, leaving behind only a few gritty pebbles. The pebbles coalesced to become the inner planets—Mercury, Venus, Earth, and Mars. Those planets are gatherings of cosmic leftovers, grains of stardust, flyspecks of the lumpish stuff that nature had contrived in the cores of stars that lived and died before the sun was born—silicon and oxygen and carbon and iron—a pinch of the universe's tiny store of solidity.

●

The Roman Catholic liturgy for the eve of Easter invokes the Canticle of Ezechiel: *I cry out until the dawn. Like a swallow I utter shrill cries; I moan like a dove.* It is a liturgy of anticipation—out of darkness the soul calls for light, out of winter the soul calls for warmth. I lie on cold sandstone slabs. My breath condenses in a hazy mist. The first migrant birds of spring flutter in the heather and furze; the curlew and the lapwing murmur and coo. The Atlantic is at my back, a huge reservoir of darkness that reaches from pole to pole. On Easter eve the altar fires are extinguished, and in darkened churches new fires are kindled, as even now a new sun is kindling in the hills beyond Dingle.

On my sandstone bed I roll with the turning Earth toward the equinoctial fire, the Paschal flame, an incandescent globe of hydrogen and helium one million miles in diameter and ninety-three million miles away. The gallery grave on Caherard Hill is oriented to the equinoxes. In this it is not unique. All across northern Europe enormous stones were raised in prehistoric times to mark the cardinal passages of the sun. Stonehenge, in Britain, is the most famous of these sites. The solar-oriented mounds in the Valley of the Boyne near Dublin are the largest. There is hardly a hilltop in Britain or Ireland that does not have its arrangement of megaliths. In a farmer's field at Lateevemore, not far from Caherard Hill, there is a monolith that stands three times taller than a man. That huge stone weighs no less than fifty tons. As nearly as I can figure it, the stone was quarried a mile away from the place where it now stands. Moving the stone and setting it erect must have placed an enormous strain upon the resources of the neolithic population of the peninsula. What was the stone's significance? Was it a sundial? Was it phallic? Was it meant to stand as the axis of the world? The sandstone monolith at Lateevemore is a shaft of compacted grains of silicon dioxide, hewn from the Earth's solid body and lifted to the sky. Every atom of the stone, every atom of silicon and oxygen, was forged in a star.

On the opposite side of Caherard Hill, at Milltown near Dingle, there is a pair of standing stones, now fallen, called the Gates of Glory. It is an impressive site, containing in addition to the megaliths of the "gate" a massive recumbent stone decorated with circular depressions—possibly sun symbols—and a third standing stone aligned with the "gate" toward the midwinter sunset. There are other outlying stones, probably marking still other astronomical alignments. Once I went to that place at dawn on Easter morning and watched the sun rise between the Gates of Glory. *He is not here, He is risen*, said the angel in gleaming garments who guarded the empty tomb of Jesus. It is a recurring theme, this murmur of resurrection; it is a theme grounded in the mystery of the world, in the mystery of light and matter, in the mystery of life and death. *Why do you seek the living among the dead?* asked the angel. *He is risen.*

Proposition 15: The diameter of the sun has to the diameter of the Earth a ratio greater than that which 19 has to 3, but less than that which 43 has to 6. The proposition is from a work of Aristarchus of Samos, who lived in the Eastern Mediterranean world around 200 B.C. The proposition states that the true diameter of the sun is more than seven times greater than the diameter of the Earth. It was one of the most startling assertions in the history of human knowing.

Aristarchus traveled, at the very least, from the island of Samos in the Aegean to Alexandria in Egypt. He sailed on voyages of many days across the broad sea. He understood that the Earth was a sphere, and he knew from minute changes in the elevations of the stars that the seemingly great distance from Samos to Alexandria was only a tiny fraction of the circumference of the Earth. He stood on the deck of a ship in the middle of the sea and imagined the huge curve of the Earth arching from horizon to horizon, and beyond the horizon to the place where arc meets arc at the back of the globe, 8,000 miles straight down beneath the keel of the ship. In the slap of waves against the ship's planks he felt the force of the great western ocean that lay beyond the Pillars of Hercules. On his face he felt the hot wind that blew from the uncrossable deserts to the south. He looked at the stars on the eastern horizon and remembered that the armies of Alexander had marched for many months to reach distant India. And he looked at the sun, that small disk of light on the dome of the sky—he could cover the disk with the tip of his little finger held at arm's length—and he saw, in his mind's eye, a globe seven times bigger than the Earth!

To have guessed that the sun was bigger than the Earth sets Aristarchus apart as one of the most imaginative thinkers of all time. It was not a wild guess or a poetic fantasy; rather, it was a matter of careful observation, mathematical deduction, and genius. Aristarchus measured the angle between the places of the sun and the moon in the sky at the time when the moon was exactly half full. On papyrus he sketched a triangle whose vertices were the Earth, the sun, and the moon. When the moon is half full, the angle with vertex at the moon is a right angle. The angle with vertex at the Earth he had measured. The third angle of the triangle and the ratios of the sides of the triangle were now determined. The sun, he calculated, was nineteen times more distant than the moon. But the sun and moon appear to be about the same size in the sky; therefore, the sun must be nineteen times bigger than the moon. Aristarchus next observed an eclipse of the moon and measured the time required for the moon to pass through the shadow of the Earth. Again, he drew circles and triangles—the sun, the Earth, the shadow of the Earth, and the moon—and with ratios and similar triangles worked out the sizes and distances of the sun and moon with respect to the size of the Earth. The sun, he saw, was seven times bigger than the Earth.

It was a *tour de force*, the most brilliant piece of scientific thinking in antiquity. It led to a conclusion so daring, so overwhelming in its implications, that no one else was ready to accept it for a thousand years. But

Aristarchus *did* accept what reason told him was true. Not only did he accept that the sun was larger than the Earth, but he followed that insight to its natural conclusion: The Earth, said Aristarchus, is not the immobile center of the universe. The larger object does not revolve about the smaller, but the other way around. The Earth revolves around the sun and rotates on its axis. The apparent rising and setting of the sun and the turning of the stars are illusions. It is the Earth that moves! It is the Earth that spins in the night like a piece of flotsam turning in the dark sea. The Earth participates in the whirl of stars.

●

Who was this man who imagined that the Earth moved? Of the life of Aristarchus of Samos we know almost nothing. He came from Samos, a Greek island near the coast of Asia Minor. He was a pupil of Strato of Lampsacus, who succeeded Theophrastus as head of the Peripatetic school in 288 B.C. That he was a capable mathematician is proved by the contents of his book *On the Sizes and Distances of the Sun and the Moon.* He also wrote on vision, light, and color, but those works have not survived. He is credited with the invention of a new type of sundial in the shape of a hemisphere marked with lines that gave directly the celestial coordinates (azimuth and elevation) of the sun. Aristarchus is best remembered for his assertion that the Earth moves in an orbit about the sun; it was a heresy that evoked the outrage of his contemporaries.

Aristarchus calculated that the sun was seven times bigger than the Earth, and it seemed to him only logical that the smaller object should revolve around the larger.

But there was a compelling argument against allowing an orbital motion to the Earth, an argument that Aristarchus was fully able to appreciate: *If the Earth moves in a circle about the sun, then our observations of the stars should be affected by that motion.* If the Earth moves on a circle about a central sun, then the *apparent* separation of two stars will be greater when the motion of the Earth takes us nearer to the stars, and less when we move away from those stars. But the apparent separations of the stars remain *absolutely constant* throughout the year, exactly as if we made our observations from a *fixed* point at the center of the universe. In order to maintain the motion of the Earth and yet explain the constancy of our observations of the stars, Aristarchus was forced to suppose that the outermost sphere of the universe, the sphere of the stars, must be extraordinarily large—so large that the *entire orbit* of the Earth is as small in relation to the sphere of the stars as a point at the center of a circle is to the circle's circumference. Not only is the sun seven times bigger than the Earth, but (according to Aristarchus) the cosmos itself is almost infinitely large compared with the Earth, the sun, and the orbit of the Earth about the sun.

Such audacity! Aristarchus rejected the cozy egglike cosmos of his contemporaries, a cosmos centered on a stable Earth and fashioned on a human scale. The sun, he claimed, is a central fire that dwarfs the Earth. The size of the universe is essentially infinite. The stars are monstrous lights at vast distances from us. Aristarchus embraced these huge celestial spaces with the courage of a Columbus embarking upon the western ocean. And once he had set sail upon this sea of infinities, where would he find safe harbor? Where was the other shore? The Earth is a fleck of dust caught in a whirlwind. The stars are remote and aloof. The gods, if they exist, are far away and oblivious to our prayers.

What sort of man has this sort of courage? Of the passions and motivations of Aristarchus we know nothing. The silence of history is unbearable. We want to ask him: *How does one lift the food to one's mouth in an infinite universe? How does one give and find love on a fleck of dust? Why get out of bed in the morning if history is only a trouble of ants?* Could the answers to these questions be found in the life of the boy growing up on the island of Samos? Did he range widely on that sun-struck island? Did he watch ships come and go from the harbor, their decks resplendent in the sunlight and their sails fat with the wind? Did he daydream in the shadows and the silence of the olive groves? Did he climb through the pine forests to the barren summit of Mount Kerkis and from that peak watch the sun rise over Asia and set in the Aegean Sea? At night, did he listen by candlelight to the story of that other native of Samos, Pythagoras, who had also dared to dream? Let Aristarchus do all of that, and then...could he tell us what it means to live on a grain of stardust?

The Lord answered Job from the whirlwind: *Have you since your birth commanded the morning, and shown the dawning of the day its place? Do you know the order of the heavens, and can you set down the reason of the Earth? Where were you when the dust was poured onto the Earth, and the clods fastened together?* The heresy of Aristarchus was the same as the sin of

Job—to have spoken of those things that exceeded his knowledge. And what a splendid heresy it was—to have reached, to have reasoned, to have dreamed. Cleanthes, the leader of the Stoic school at Athens, urged the Greeks to indict Aristarchus for impiety. Insofar as we know, Aristarchus escaped that fate. He went on searching for the order of the heavens and for the place of the dawning of the day.

It turns out that Aristarchus was wrong about the size of the sun. The sun is not seven times bigger than the Earth; it is actually more than one hundred times bigger! Aristarchus calculated that three hundred Earths would fit within the body of the sun; the correct figure is closer to one million. The error was not in his method, or in his reasoning, or in the reach of his imagination. The error was in the making of certain crucial observations, observations for which no satisfactory instruments existed at his time.

Although the sun is a million times more voluminous than the Earth, the ratio of the masses is only a third of that. The sun is mostly hydrogen and helium; the Earth is mostly oxygen, silicon, and iron. Five billion years ago, in the condensing presolar nebula, a dust of sand and iron was poured upon the Earth—gathered to the Earth by gravity—and the clods adhered together. Whirling motions of the nebula were transferred to the accreting Earth, so that the Earth spun with a double motion about the new sun. The surface of the Earth was alternately exposed to day and night, to summer and winter. In the heat and violence of the planet's formation it acquired an envelope of gases and steam; and when the planet cooled, the steam condensed and fell as rain that collected in the rocky hollows of the crust. At some point, nearly four billion years ago, life appeared in the sun-warmed seas in the form of single-celled organisms. Out of radiance had come solidity; out of solidity, life.

And the Lord spoke from the whirlwind: *The waters are hardened like stone, and the surface of the deep is congealed. Were you there, in the depths of the sea? When the gates of death were opened, did you see the darksome doors?* All around me this morning on Caherard Hill there are the sounds of life waiting for the sun. The grasses sing in it, the valley wells up with it—warbles, pipings, chitters, whistles, squawks, bellows, bleats, and mewings. In that unsilent silence, I hear my own breathing, heavy with anticipation, heaving like the sea. I lie on a bed of stone and watch and wait for the sun to rise beyond Dingle, beyond the darksome doors, beyond the Gates of Glory.

How, I wonder, did Aristarchus answer the charge of impiety? Cleanthes accused him of putting the hearth of the universe into motion. Did Aristarchus reply that the radiant sun is a more appropriate hearth for the universe than the darksome Earth? Did he answer that the votive fire is the proper center for the temple, rather than the mote of dust that dances in its light? The heresy of Aristarchus was the heresy of scale, like the heresy of Job and the heresy of Galileo. Aristarchus dared to suggest that the creation was not measured on a human scale. And yet, in his works, the human imagination stretched to encompass an infinite creation. The bold theorems of Aristarchus are prayers that address the infinity of the world; his mathematical propositions are the language of praise. When the waters were hardened like stone and when the surface of the deep was congealed, he was there, *praising.*

The curlew is one of the first seasonal migrants to return to the west of Ireland. It is, as they say, an "instinct bird," like the cuckoo and the swift, and sets its course northward from Africa by the calendar date rather than the weather. (Starlings and skylarks, on the other hand, are "weather birds," sometimes tempted north by a premature spell of felicitous weather, only to find themselves in trouble when the season takes a turn for the worse.) As I wait for the sun on Caherard Hill a curlew flaps up from the furze; it is probably a transient, rather than one of a mating pair. Curlews are attracted to high, boggy places and are at home on the hilltops where neolithic peoples built their sun-pointing graves. The curlew flutters up and then glides smoothly down, its long curving beak slicing the air like a scimitar. I listen to its flutelike whistles and trills. It knows—as I know— that the year is poised this morning on the knife-edge of the equinox, and that from this day forward the sun will commence its slow progress back toward summer's end of the beam.

Five billion years ago, the Earth condensed from a whirling eddy of dust and gas in the circling nebula that became our solar system. Within the larger whirlpool there was a smaller whirlpool of hydrogen and helium

and oxygen and silicon and iron. The heavier elements in that sub-whirlpool collected into a knot, and the ignition of the new sun (at the center of the larger whirlpool) blew the lighter elements away. The knot was spinning in a way that was by chance somewhat askew to the plane of the larger whirlpool. Or perhaps the young Earth was knocked akilter by collision with another object. However it happened, the Earth now spins on an axis that is tipped to the plane of the orbit by twenty-three-and-a-half degrees. It was happenstance. The tilt was the luck of the draw. Out of the random shuffle of its creation, the Earth drew a tip of twenty-three-and-a-half degrees. It could have been thirty; it could have been zero. But it was twenty-three-and-a-half degrees, and on almost every hilltop in Ireland there are heavy stones set up to commemorate that fact.

If there were not a tip to the axis of the Earth, there would be no seasons. The curlew would not *even now* be testing the temper of the air. The stones on which I lie would not *even now* be adjusting the restlessness of their molecules to the quickening tempo of the equinoctial dawn, a warming and an agitation that day by day has been accumulating in every atomic bond and interstice. It is because of the tip of the Earth's axis that the sun is sometimes in the northern sky and sometime in the southern sky, and there is a following terrestrial tide of force and vitality that flows north and south with the sun. The sun swings back and forth in the sky, and a huge energy surges on the surface of the Earth, north to south, south to north, like water sloshing in a tipped bowl.

Since the earliest days of Christendom, the feast of Easter has been appointed for the first Sunday after the full moon following the equinox. The full moon after the equinox is called the Grass Moon or the Egg Moon. The setting of the date for Easter was a canonical statement both solar and lunar. Easter is the feast of the restored sun, of new life, and of resurrection. It is the equinoctial feast. The energy that *even now* is gathering in the hills beyond Dingle is the energy of sap and blood. In a moment, the sun will wet the hilltops with its fluid light. The standing stone at Lateevemore will cast a long phallic shadow to the west. *And behold, at dawn, there was a great earthquake: for the angel of the Lord descended from heaven, and came and rolled back the stone from the door of the tomb, and sat upon it. His countenance was like lightning, and his garments were as white as snow.*

◑

There is no more perfect time of the day than these last few moments before sunrise. On Caherard Hill it is as if the whole Earth is holding its breath. The stars have vacated the sky. The crescendo of light in the east has reached a volume and a pitch that can sustain no more growth without breaking like a wave. The bright waters of Ventry Harbour hush. The wind whispers. A poem comes to mind, the poem called *The Song of Amergin*, traditionally considered to be the first verse made in Ireland: *I am the wind on the sea. I am the ocean wave. I am the sound of the billows.* Not a poem, really, but a prayer, the prayer of the people who made the bed of stone on Caherard Hill. *I am the seven-horned stag. I am the hawk on the cliff. I am the dewdrop in sunlight.*

All over Ireland on this equinoctial morning, the light of the rising sun will be defined and shaped by megaliths. There are 600 megalithic graves in Ireland. On the highest peak of the Loughcrew Mountains in County Meath, there is a cairn of stone that will admit this morning into its deepest recesses a beam of sunlight that is twenty-five feet long. As the sun clears the horizon, a rectangle of yellow light will briefly fall upon the face of a stone at the back of the monument's innermost gallery; and where the light falls, the stone is decorated with an image of the sun, a flowerlike pattern of circles and petals. At Knowth, in the Valley of the Boyne, there is a monument with a tunnel one hundred feet long that is aligned to the rising of the equinoctial sun. That massive heap of earth and stones was created sometime around 3700 B.C. It is older than the pyramids of Egypt. It is called the Cave of the Sun.

I wait now, afraid to take my eyes from the horizon. In the fields, slugs tarry in their slow progression. Cuckoos bate their morning song. Who was Amergin, that first poet? *I am the fairest of flowers. I am the raging boar. I am the salmon in the deep pool. I am the lake on the plain.* Legend says that Amergin was the brother of Evir, Ir, and Eremon, Milesian princes who colonized Ireland many hundreds of years before the birth of Christ. I try to imagine myself standing with the four brothers on Caherard Hill, waiting for sunrise. Waiting for what? For the petaled fire. For the heat that animates. For the light that awakens. Do we stand here as dumb as stones? Are our hearts as cold as the sandstone slabs of the Giant's Bed? Not likely. The poet exclaims: *I am the meaning of the poem. I am the point of the spear. I am the god that makes fire in the head.*

And now the light comes in ripples over Brandon Mountain, and the dark hills burn. A sliver of the sun appears on the crest of the distant range; the sliver of light is disconnected from the sun's still-hidden disk, pared away from the body of the sun by a trick of refraction. Suddenly Dingle Bay is burnished like a shield. Stones shine in the dewy grass. *Who levels the mountain? Who announces the age of the moon? Who has been where the sun sleeps? Who?* asks Amergin, *if not I.*

I am up on my elbows, and the sliver of the new sun is perched upon my toes. That red shimmering light is ninety-three million miles away, eight light-minutes away. Almost instantly, the sliver becomes reattached to the body of the sun. Now the full solar disk mushrooms from the ridge, fattening until it balances on the skyline like a rolling wheel. The rising takes two minutes—two minutes for the Earth to turn on its axis one-half of a degree. I am flying toward the sun on my bed of stone at a thousand miles per hour. Two minutes from the first instant of dawn and it is fully day. All over Ireland salmon stir in their deep pools. The fair sea pinks shake in their sea-cliff hollows. And suddenly there is a huge booming noise, like a crack of thunder, and my first thought is that I have actually *heard* the sunrise, heard the wrenching report of the sun as it let go of the horizon. I quickly realize that what I have just heard had nothing to do with the sun. It was a sonic boom—a military jet, perhaps, on an early-morning flight to America. But somewhere in the mountains near the foot of Dingle Bay a hawk lets go of its perch and falls onto rising air, even as I fall toward the place on the horizon that has disgorged the sun. *Who?* asks Amergin. And who, indeed, if not I?

PRIME

In the Treasure House of Snow

FOR SIXTEEN YEARS I have been a student of the Irish weather. I have studied the daily weather maps in the *Irish Times*. I have listened to the six o'clock shipping forecasts on the BBC, the daily litany of reports from coastal weather stations—Malin Head, Shannon, Valencia, Fastnet—*especially* Valencia, that battleship of gray rock that lies on the horizon outside my window. I have watched the barometer. I have held a moistened finger to the wind. And what have I learned? That two forecasts will serve for 90 percent of the time: "Wet almost everywhere with sunny intervals" or "Mostly dry with occasional showers." The remaining 10 percent of Irish weather includes winter gales that blow from Iceland with a force that withers trees and rattles the tiles on the roof, and summer anticyclones that drift up from the Azores to sit for days upon Ireland like sunny crowns.

Ireland's weather comes from the Atlantic. It is a rare wind that makes its way across the Irish Sea from Britain. The weather maps published daily by the Irish Meteorological Office show Ireland near the right-hand margin of the maps, and we can assume only that whatever happens east of the island is irrelevant. On the left-hand margin of the maps is Labrador. The blank space in between is the North Atlantic, a notorious weather generator. In that wet arena south of Greenland, cool air from the Arctic and tropical air from Bermuda are in constant conflict. When these unstable air masses collide, they generate depression after depression that are hurled eastward toward Ireland. It is not unusual for two fronts to pass over the country in a single day. A day that begins in mist and drizzle can end in brilliant sunshine. A day that begins calm and bright can end with a gale. And the only way to tell what the weather will be like tomorrow is to look out of the window when you wake up.

When I looked out of the window this morning, on the first day of the new year, there was a surprise. The close-cropped fields and the yellow strand were dusted with snow! The flanks of Mount Eagle (the peak itself was still in cloud) were blanketed with white. Most winters I am a New Englander, and on New Year's Day I am usually up to my knees in snow; but snow in Ireland is rare, even in January, and especially here on the southwest coast. Ireland is warmed by the Gulf Stream, an ocean river that carries the heat of Mexico 4,000 miles

north and east to the shores of Europe; if you stand on my doorstep and face the prevailing wind you can catch a whiff of rain forest and enchiladas. Ireland is at the latitude of Labrador, but its winter climate is more like South Carolina's. There is rarely enough snow to be a nuisance in Dublin, in the east of the island, and snow is almost unheard of in the southwest. Palm trees grow in Cork and Kerry, and fuchsia, a temperate import from southern latitudes, runs rank in those counties like a weed. The snow on the flanks of Mount Eagle this morning was an unexpected gift. It came on a stray wind from the Arctic. I brewed a quick cup of coffee and laced on my boots. I knew the snow would not survive the morning sun.

●

From Ventry the most convenient route to the summit of Mount Eagle is up the macadam road to the little village of Kildurrihy. The village, with its score of houses and two holy wells, sits just at the change of slope where cultivated fields give way to mountain pasturage. From the village, a rough track leads at a reckless sort of angle right up the mountain to a lake that is set in a dark glacial cirque. It is from this lake that the parish obtains its supply of fresh water. And at the lake I enter the cloud that cloaks the mountain's summit and shivers out dry white flakes onto winter grass and heather.

North of the lake, a narrow switchback path climbs the steep face of the headwall cliffs. It is an old donkey path, laboriously cut into the slope, that in earlier times gave the farmers of Kildurrihy access to the turf cuttings on the mountain's shoulder. After several sharp switchbacks I stop to rest. The parish has vanished! The lake too has vanished, although I can still hear the slap of water on the shore, amplified by the precipitous walls of the cirque. I put out my arm and wiggle my fingers; they are like parts of someone else's body out there in the cloud. While my arm is extended, snowflakes settle onto the dark cloth of my sleeve. The flakes had their origin high overhead, in cold supersaturated air at the top of the storm. The crystals began their growth on a nucleus of wind-borne dust (every snowflake has at its center an invisible grain of dust, a heart of stone), and fell once, twice, three times, or more, gathering weight, and were lifted again and again by updrafts of the easterly wind, each time acquiring new dendretic fingerings, branchings, featherings. Each of the crystals is perfect and astonishingly symmetrical. Hans Castorp, on Thomas Mann's *Magic Mountain*, found snowflakes upon *his* sleeve, too—"little jewels, insignia, orders, agraffes," he called them, "uncannily anti-organic, life-denying, icily regular in form." For Castorp, the rigid symmetry of the snowflakes was terrifying. But I know what Hans Castorp could not have known (because when Thomas Mann invented that *other* snowstorm on that *other* mountain, science had not yet probed the interior of the ice crystal), that the snowflake is more than a life-denying hexagon of solid water. The snowflake is icily regular, but it is also chaotic; it is the seal of Abel *and* the mark of Cain, a dactylogram of the eternal conflict between order and disorder that rages at the heart of creation.

On New Year's Day in 1610, the astronomer Johannes Kepler presented his patron, John Wacker, Counsellor to the Imperial Court, a little book entitled *The Six-*

Cornered Snowflake. It was a New Year's gift. It was also the first recorded step toward a mathematical theory of natural form.

Why, asks Kepler in his little treatise, do snowflakes fall as six-cornered starlets, "tufted like feathers"? There must be a *cause,* he asserts, for if it happens by chance, then why don't snowflakes fall with five corners or with seven? Casting about for an answer, Kepler considers other hexagons in nature: the shape of the cell in a honcycomb, for example. He shows that a hexagonal architecture for the honeycomb exactly suits the bee's purpose, for (as Kepler proves) the hexagon is the geometrical figure that enables the bee to enclose a maximum volume of honey with a minimum of wax. (It is a matter of the ratios of the areas of plane geometric figures to their perimeters and the sharing of sides between space-filling polygons, mathematical problems that Kepler found easy to solve.) Next Kepler considers the seeds of the pomegranate, which are also hexagonal in form. He demonstrates that this is the shape any round, pliable object will take if a mass of such objects is squeezed equally from every side into a minimal volume, as the seeds of the pomegranate are squeezed together in the growing fruit. (Kepler's discussion of pomegranate seeds anticipates what modern crystallographers call the mathematics of "close-packing.") Then Kepler reviews other possible "causes" for the snowflake's six-sided elegance: formal causes, teleological causes, efficient causes. He considers the role of beauty, function, and necessity. Perhaps, Kepler muses somewhat whimsically, like Olympian athletes snowflakes take care "not to fall in an ugly or immodest fashion." Or maybe, he concludes, in making snowflakes, nature simply "plays."

By inverting my pocket binoculars, I can magnify the snowflakes on my sleeve, but I must be quick about it, for even in the cold air the heat of my body soon melts the flakes. It is easy to see why Kepler could imagine that nature "plays." The snowflakes are like the patterns in a child's kaleidoscope. They have the same playful balance of stasis and variation that are found in a child's rhyme ("Here is the house that Jack built. Here is the malt that lay in the house..."). But Kepler knew that "play" cannot be the entire story. At the end of his little book, Kepler confesses his ignorance and leaves the problem of the snowflake's symmetry to future generations of natural philosophers.

The riddle of the snowflake has since been partly solved. Physicists have traced the snowflake's six-sided secret down into the heart of matter, to the form of the water molecule, and, ultimately, to the laws of atomic bonding that give the water molecule its shape. A water molecule consists of an oxygen atom that is linked with two atoms of hydrogen. The hydrogens are attached to the oxygen at the same sort of angle as the left-hand prongs of this letter X. The water molecule has two other "arms" of electric charge, like the right-hand prongs of the X, but twisted in the third dimension. These "free arms" establish links with other molecules of water. The geometry of the arms ensures that when water molecules link up to form a crystal of ice, they arrange themselves in a regular hexagonal lattice (just as the octagonal arrangement of the holes in the knobs of a Tinker Toy set determine the eight-fold symmetry of the structures that can be built with the knobs and sticks). The snowflake is six-sided because the angle between the arms of the water molecule is approximately the same as the interior angle of a hexagon; any other pattern of symmetry would require that the water molecules be bent out of shape.

Kepler would be pleased to know that the beauty of the snowflake is founded upon principles of mathematical order. He would have been surprised to learn that atoms play a role in the explanation. Kepler rejected atomism because he assumed that a rattling, clattering chaos of Democritean atoms could never give rise to the elegant symmetries of nature. But if twentieth-century physics has taught us anything, it is that nature accommodates beautiful form even at the level of the atom. Beauty in nature is not something that shows up only at a certain level of complexity, like the Palladian beauty of a Monticello built of featureless bricks. Beauty is built into every jot and tittle of creation—into every atomic brick! Beauty soaks reality as water fills a rag. "Hast thou entered into the treasure-house of the snow?" the Lord asked Job from the whirlwind. Beauty is the treasure. Beauty is banked and counted upon my sleeve.

As I climb the switchback path, the cloud climbs too. Occasionally the base of the cloud lifts above my head and I catch a glimpse of the dark lake lying passive in its sandstone bowl, and farther down the stone-strewn, snow-powdered slope lies the village of Kildurrihy. A single square mile of Dingle Bay shines in sunlight; there is a hole out there in the clouds—the storm is breaking up. Sheep scurry from my path, oblivious to the storm; their thick winter fleeces are dusted with snow and splashed with red and blue identifying dyes. We are apparently out of place here, the sheep and I, like Hans Castorp in the storm on the Magic Mountain.

The glacial cirque is an unrelentingly inorganic corner of the universe, a cold, gray harbor of quartz, ice, and flakes of snow, each flake containing at its heart a tiny invisible particle of kaolinite or montmorillonite, meteoric dust, or volcanic ash. The laws that rule the mountain's face are the laws of prisms and plates, graupel and rimed crystal—geometrical laws, spare and steady. There are probably whole planets like this in the universe, breathless and bloodless, shivering in the embrace of the snowflake's cold symmetry.

Has the mystery of the snowflake, then, been entirely plumbed? Certainly not! Physicists are content that they can explain the hexagonal symmetry of the crystals, but they can say very little about the delicacy of the branching and the extraordinary congruity of the six points. For these things science has provided only the beginning of an understanding. It is clear that particles of airborne dust provide the nuclei about which snowflake crystals begin to grow. Without dust there would be no snow. Once the growth has begun, water molecules attach themselves to the nucleus in ways that yield the lowest free energy. Low free energy, in the scheme of nature, corresponds to high structural symmetry. The snowflake's free energy is at rock bottom, which is why the snowflake is a paradigm of symmetry. But the appar-

ent *stability* of the ice crystal, like the apparent fixity of the mountain, is an illusion. Careful studies have shown that on the atomic scale the snowflake is a frenzy of activity. The molecules of water furiously swing their hydrogen arms like dancers in a tarantella. The electronic bonds between the molecules are made and broken a million times a second. Faults in the crystal—places where there are extra hydrogen atoms or missing atoms— jump from place to place like unruly children in a teacherless classroom. And somehow, in the midst of this atomic caprice, the snowflake acquires and retains an ordered form. We are in the face of one of nature's most profound mysteries: how beauty and structure arise from a delicate balance of order and disorder.

Kepler hoped to find in the six-cornered snowflake the *facultas formatrix* of nature—the formative capacity that brings beauty into being. The twentieth-century physicist looks for that formative capacity in the interplay of energy and entropy, those bedrock principles of physics, principles as gray and bare, as fundamental and enduring, as the rocky face of Mount Eagle. The growth of snow crystals has been modeled by physicists on computers. The laws of energy and entropy are programmed into the model, and the rest is left to the throw of the dice (a random number generator is built into the program). Simulated molecules are allowed to randomly migrate toward a simulated crystal and attach themselves to the growing aggregate in ways that minimize the energy of the system. The resulting crystal is displayed on the computer's screen. The electronic simulations yield snowflakes with a crude hexagonal symmetry, but with nothing like the perfect six-fold congruency of real snowflakes. The remarkable symmetry of *real* crystals must be the consequence of some cooperative phenomenon involving the entire crystal, something that has not yet been incorporated into the models. But what can it be? How can one face of the growing crystal know what is happening on another face? On the scale of molecules, one part of the snowflake's growing perimeter is separated from another by "light-years." Physicists can only guess at how symmetry is maintained across the whole crystal as molecules of water attach themselves at random around the crystal's growing edge. Some physicists think that *vibrations* of the crystalline lattice are the instrument of communication, vibrations that are exquisitely sensitive to the shape of the crystal. If this is so, then the growing snowflake maintains its symmetry in the same way that members of an orchestra stay in consonance, by sharing the sound of the ensemble. The snowflake's beauty, then, is orchestral! The *facultas formatrix* is vibration. Nature shudders in its sublimity. Atoms dance to inaudible music. The cloud jams. The rock jives. The lake's still surface boogie-woogies.

I have a friend who speaks of knowledge as an island in a sea of mystery. It is a lovely image. Let this, then, be the ground of my faith: *All that we know, now and forever, all scientific knowledge that we have of this world, or ever will have, is as an island in the sea.* Say what you can about minimum free energy, increasing entropy, lattice vibrations, and crystal symmetry; say all that you can about atoms, and valencies, and hydrogen bonds; calculate with exquisite finesse the quantum mechanical wave function of a single electron in a crystal of ice; and still the snowflake will rebuke our ignorance.

We live in our partial knowledge as the Dutch live on polders claimed from the sea. We dike and fill. We dredge up soil from the bed of mystery and build ourselves room to grow. And still the mystery surrounds us. It laps at our shores. It permeates the land. Scratch the surface of knowledge and mystery bubbles up like a spring. And, occasionally, at certain disquieting moments in history (Aristarchus, Galileo, Planck, and Einstein), a tempest of mystery comes rolling in from the sea and overwhelms our efforts, reclaims knowledge that has been built up by years of patient work, and forces us to retreat to the surest, most secure core of what we know, where we huddle in fear and trembling until the storm subsides, and then we start building again, throwing up dikes, pumping, filling, extending the perimeter of our knowledge and our security.

At the end of his essay on the snowflake, Kepler confesses that he has merely "knocked on the door of knowledge." As a physicist, I have studied what four centuries of investigation have added to Kepler's pioneering work, and still every snowflake upon my sleeve is a cipher. If I pursue the mystery down into the atoms of the crystal lattice, or up into the wind that blows against the sandstone face of the mountain, the mystery remains—all-abiding, undepleted, inexplicable. What I have learned about the physics of crystalline structures does not lessen the mystery of the snowflake; it grounds it in a deeper, broader mystery that envelops my partial knowledge as the cloud envelops the mountain, as the sea envelops the land. The mystery of the snowflake participates in the rock and the wind. It hides in the mountain as Behemoth hides in the bowels of the Earth, and it hides in the cloud as Leviathan hides in the sea. Behemoth resided in every grain of rock and iron of which the Earth was made; Leviathan was there four billion years ago when the waters were congealed in the deep. The plates of Behemoth and the scales of Levithan are here upon my sleeve, six-sided, lovely in their symmetry. I can tell you the number of molecules in each flake of snow. I know nothing.

◗

The snowflake is an emblem of order in nature; it is also an insignia of disorder. It is an artifact of law and an artifact of chaos. It arises out of vapors in the air with a fixed symmetry and with infinite variation. Every snow-flake is alike, and every snowflake is different. In the snowflake, if it is to be found at all, is an adequate image for the *facultas formatrix* that resides in the rock and in the air.

But can it *really* be true, as we have often heard, that no two snowflakes are alike? Can the random casting of nature's dice so overwhelm the rule of law? There was never anyone better able to answer that question from direct experience than Wilson A. Bentley. Bentley was a New England farmer and an amateur meteorologist. For fifty years he observed flakes of snow. In the course of his lifetime he photographed 5,000 snowflakes. He never found two alike.

Bentley was born in 1865 near Jericho, Vermont. He had almost no formal schooling, but his mother was a schoolteacher, and from her he acquired a lively curiosity and a love for nature's minutiae. Drops of water, bits of stone, the feathers of birds, and tiny insects equally excited his interest. By the time he was eight years old he had made a collection of almost every species of fern that grew in Vermont. Even then he was on the track of the *facultas formatrix.*

Wilson Bentley's mother owned books, including a set of encyclopedias; he read them all. Her finest gift to her son was an old microscope that she gave to the boy on his fifteenth birthday. It was snowing that day, and Bentley succeeded in glimpsing a six-sided snowflake with the instrument. That glimpse was a revelation; he had seen for an instant into the treasure house of snow; in the fleeting moment before the snowflake melted, he had been where the waters were congealed and had walked in the lowest parts of the deep; he had observed Behemoth, with bones like brass and a tail of cedar; he had seen Leviathan, who drinks the River Jordan. Do I exaggerate? It is, of course, impossible to know what Bentley saw that day through the eyepiece of his mother's microscope, but we know it excited a passion that never subsided.

At the age of twenty, the unschooled farm boy had perfected a technique for photographing snow crystals. When death ended the adventure half a century later, Wilson Bentley had accumulated thousands of micro-photographs of snowflakes. He had acquired worldwide fame as an expert on the meteorology of snow. In his own neighborhood, in the mountains of Vermont, he was known simply as "the Snowflake Man." An editorial in the *Burlington Free Press* on the day after his death said this: "He saw something in the snowflakes which other men failed to see, not because they could not see, but because they had not the patience and the understanding to look."

Bentley was a man of science. He was fully aware that his marvelous photographs were a unique and invaluable contribution to the sciences of crystallography and meteorology. Each photographic plate was a tiny addition to the high ground of knowledge claimed from mystery. Sets of prints made from his glass-plate negatives were distributed to museums and schools at home and abroad. Even today, one can hardly pick up an article or book on the crystallography of snow that does not contain one or more of Bentley's photographs. But Bentley's passion was grounded in something more than knowledge; he never lost sight of the ambient mystery. In every crystal of snow he recognized something beyond knowledge, beyond the province of reason. What he saw was a foundation for order and variation "more beautiful than ever [was] pictured in our dreams, or in our most extravagant flights of fancy."

We have Bentley's word for it that no two snowflakes in his collection were alike. That fact was a source of satisfaction for him. In the snowflake he stood face to face with nature's deepest mystery. The Greeks called it the mystery of *the One and the Many:* How does form endure in the face of almost limitless possibility? The snowflake exemplified for Bentley the kaleidoscopic balance of order and disorder that is the basis for all beauty in art and in nature.

At the top of the steep headwall of the glacial cirque, the switchback path levels out onto a turf-banked shoulder of Mount Eagle. I walk between the rich black walls of fresh turf cuttings, shaped and stepped into a kind of crystalline order by the slice of the spade. Turf is no longer removed from the mountain in donkey baskets down the narrow lakeside path; rather, a road has been bulldozed up the back side of the mountain, and tractors pulling carts drive directly into the cuttings, to be loaded at the ricks where the turf has been set to dry in the sun. The cloud has lifted, and the sun that earlier glazed a single square mile of Dingle Bay now breaks full upon glittering water. The turf cuttings are suddenly transformed into a world of vertical black and horizontal white, a stepped checkerboard of peat and snow, the one simmering in the gentle heat of its slow organic combustion, the other readily yielding its icy organic symmetry to the sun. I look down into the black bowl of the lake, and beyond to the green and brown fields (already bare of snow) that reach to Kildurrihy, brilliant now in sunlight. There is a dramatic change in temperature. I strip off my jacket and march up the snow-covered slope to the summit of the mountain.

Wilson Bentley examined 5,000 snowflakes and found no two alike. But 5,000 is a small number. I could bend down and scoop up 5,000 flakes in my hand. What if I had the patience to examine five million snowflakes, or five billion, or every snowflake on Mount Eagle; then would I find two alike? The question can be given an answer, and the answer is a resounding *no*. Once I melted a cupful of snowflakes; it yielded ten cubic centimeters of water, or ten grams. A single snow crystal weighs about a millionth of a gram. That means there were ten million snowflakes in the cup. The snow on Mount Eagle this morning is about a "cup" deep. A cup has an area of about twenty square centimeters, and the mountain an area of twenty square kilometers. Putting all of this together, I calculate that about one billion cups of snow have fallen this morning onto Mount Eagle; that's ten quadrillion snowflakes. In a similar way, I once estimated that as many as 10^{33} ("one" followed by thirty-three zeros) snow-flakes have fallen onto the face of the planet during its four-and-a-half-billion-year history. Could it really be that among that almost unimaginably large number of snowflakes no two have been alike?

Turn to the possibilities of combination. A deck of fifty-two cards can be shuffled into 10^{68} different combinations, far more combinations than the number of snowflakes on the mountain. A small Tinker Toy set may have a hundred sticks and knobs; consider, if you will, the huge number of different structures that could be built with such a set (all of them with the octagonal symmetry determined by the holes in the knobs). A single flake of snow consists of something like 10^{18} (one quintillion) molecules of water! As the snowflake grows, molecules attach themselves to the growing crystal essentially at random, although guided by requirements of energy, entropy, and the exquisitely sensitive vibrations of the crystal lattice. The number of ways that 10^{18} molecules can be arranged into symmetrical six-sided crystals is astronomical, vastly larger than the number of snowflakes that have ever fallen onto the face of the Earth. The odds are very great indeed that no two snowflakes have ever been exactly identical.

The staggering diversity of snowflakes is a measure of nature's potential for novelty and change. The constancy of the snowflake's six-sided form is reassurance that nature is ruled by fixed law. Wilson Bentley once wrote: "The farm folks, up in this north country, dread the winter; but I was always supremely happy, from the day of the first snowfall—which usually came in November—until the last one, which sometimes came as late as May." For Bentley, snow was a continuing lesson

in the way nature's beauty arises from a delicate balance
of order and chaos, fixity and change. Each flake was like
a seashell or a sand dollar cast up on a sandy shore,
bearing in its flutes and symmetries intimations of mystery and hints of the surrounding sea.

The summit of the mountain is an island, broad and
flat in a sea of elements. From where I stand near the
Ordinance Survey cairn that marks the highest elevation
of Mount Eagle, there is not a single human habitation to
be seen. The parishes at the foot of the mountain—Ventry
to the east, Dunquin to the west, Ballyferriter to the
north—are sunk from sight below the brow of the hill. I
am alone in a silence as pure as any I have know. The
storm has retreated into the fastness of the Atlantic, and
the sun burns up the snow with a slanting New Year's
heat, turning flakes to crusty rime. I am in a world of
Greek elements—earth, water, air, and fire—each pure
and separate, layered and unmingling, as in a medieval
cosmological diagram—mountain, sea, sky, and sun. And
I feel, more intensely than ever before, the anomaly of
myself, the extraordinary out-of-placeness of an organic,
sentient being in this elemental world ruled by law and
chaos.

"Let him kiss me with the kiss of his mouth," says
Bernard of Clairvaux, quoting the *Song of Songs*. I would
have that kiss, at this moment of isolation and anticipation. Bernard asked for the kiss of God's mouth as
Meister Eckart asked for "the taste of God." It was not a
vague abstraction they sought, no thing that could be
caught in words; it was a being taken possession by and a
partaking of—ineffable, immediate, passionate. *Stay me*

up with flowers, compass me about with apples, sings the Bride in the Song of Songs, *because I languish with love.*

Knowledge is an island. The larger we make that island, the longer becomes the shore where knowledge is lapped by mystery. It is the most common of all misconceptions about science that it is somehow inimical to mystery, that it grows at the expense of mystery and intrudes with its brash certitudes upon the space of God. Aristarchus and Galileo felt the harsh consequences of that misconception. But in a world described by science, mystery abides, in the space between the stars and in the interstices of snow. The extension of knowledge is the extension of mystery. It is as Bernard says: "As a bee bears both honey and wax, so He has in himself both that which ignites the light of knowledge and that which infuses the taste of grace."

I am the flower of the field, and the lily of the valley, sings the Bride. *My beloved is gone down into his garden, to the bed of aromatical spices, to feed in the garden, and to gather lilies.* The garden is here, this morning, on this mountain. The garden is the lake and the sandstone ledge. The garden is the molecule of water that hangs in the air, and the grain of dust at the heart of the flake of snow. The garden is the heat of the solstitial winter sun. The garden is the mountain upon which, at this moment, I am utterly alone, with the taste of spices upon my lips.

In Thomas Mann's *Doctor Faustus*, old Jonathan Leverkuhn studies the ice crystals that have formed on the window of his farmhouse. "I should like to say," he muses, "that [the frost crystals] would have been good and belonging to the regular order of things if only the phenomena had kept to a symmetrical patter, as they ought, strictly regular and mathematical. But they did not. Impudently, deceptively, they imitated the vegetable kingdom: most prettily of all, fern fronds, grasses, the calyxes and corollas of flowers. To the utmost of their icy ability they dabbled in the organic." Do the ice crystals on Leverkuhn's window mimic the fern, or does the living frond mimic the frost? The old gentleman concludes: "Creatively dreaming Nature dreamed here and there the same dream."

Like all dreams, the dream of nature arises out of order and disorder, out of stasis and flux. It is the dream of the perennially mysterious *facultas formatrix*. The Earth formed five billion years ago from a nebula of gas and dust, and that was a dream. Much of the gas was molecular—paired atoms of hydrogen and helium, and promiscuous oxygen in combination with hydrogen, silicon, and nitrogen. There were nickel and iron, and tiny quantities of the other elements. The heavier elements accreted to form a sphere 8,000 miles in diameter, and that was a dream. Astronomers have tried to model on computers the physics of planet formation. They program into the computer the laws of gravity, and thermodynamics, and magneto-hydrodynamics, and a random number generator to simulate the essentially statistical nature of the laws of physics (as applied to complex systems), and they let the computer run, day and night, spinning out planets, dreaming imaginary solar systems. And what the computer dreams are planet systems very much like our own, with more or less the same distribution of planets, in size and composition, and the same scattering of moons. The computer-generated solar systems are alike—as snowflakes are alike—and yet different one from the other—as snowflakes are different. If the computer models accurately reflect the real world, then out there among the stars there are a billion billion planet systems and no two are alike, yet all are alike in some way. And *this* planet, this one on which I stand, in *this* solar system, this planet Earth near this yellow star, this frost-rimed island of rock and sea and sky near a warming sun, is distinguished from all of the others only in that it is mine. There may be as many planets in the universe as there are snowflakes on the mountain, and this one planet is mine. It was already there, five billion years ago, in the atoms of the interstellar nebula out of which it was born, as the snowflake exists in the mist in the air and in the grain of dust about which it accretes. The planet was dreamed as the snowflake was dreamed, out of order and disorder, out of the rule of law and the chaos of variation. The mountain was there in the nebula. And the wind. And the snowflake. And I was there.

TERCE

Abracadabra

YESTERDAY, while sorting through piles of old books in search of something misplaced, I stopped to browse through a paperback *Walden* from college days. There I rediscovered the delightful word *tantivy*. "With a slight tantivy and tremulous motion of the elm tree tops," wrote Thoreau in the chapter on the bean field. The word was marked with a red check, a faded reminder to look up the meaning. And now, thirty years later, I can remember the two words I found together on the page of the dictionary: *tantivy*, "a fast and furious gallop," and *tantara*, "a fanfare on trumpet or horn."

Only etymologists can say how those two words, of different origins, came to gallop in tandem down the page of my dictionary, but I recall the sense of profound surprise I experienced when I found them there. Tantivy! Tantara! They were vigorous words, high-spirited words—pell-mell, helter-skelter, hell-for-leather words— and their lively conjunction on the page appeared to be more than a coincidence. If I recall rightly, the discovery of those two conjoined words was my first inkling of the magic that can flow from a pen. Words, it seemed, were more than arbitrary squiggles on a page, and letters more than parallelepipeds of cold metal in a printer's tray. Words and letters are amulets, hex signs, potions, and philters; with them, one could cast spells, jinx, curse, charm, and enchant.

Tantivy! Yes, it really does affect the treetops. Even now, as I write the word, the curtains seem to rustle at the windows. In all of my schooling no one had told me that language has this power that goes beyond mere communication. Be concise, my teachers said, be correct, be clear. Dot your *i*'s and cross your *t*'s. Mind your *p*'s and *q*'s. *Dear Aunt Sally*, we were asked to write over and over, with broad, disciplined sweeps of the hand, *thank you for the red sweater*. And all the while—*tantara!*—trumpeters galloped unheard in my dictionary. There was a time when words were thought to possess a literal power over things. Ali Baba opened doors with incantatory syllables. *"Hoc est"* evoked a transubstantiation, turned bread and wine into flesh and blood. We have lost that magic in the tongue. With a sophistication befitting the inventors of the telegraph, we have reduced *hoc est* to hocus-pocus and abracadabra to dots and dashes. I did not learn the magic of language in school. Like most children of the twentieth century, I was taught spelling but not spells.

That trip to the dictionary in search of *tantivy* was a kind of epiphany, an invitation into the ancient cabala of language, an initiation into anagoge. I began to read the dictionary the way a Rosicrucian might search the Scriptures for secret meanings. Surely it is no accident, I thought, that *plums* are linked by *p*'s and *u*'s to *plump*, *purple, pluck, pinch,* and *spurt.* As I learned such spells, plums were transformed, and simple experience became poetry. It was not long before I fell under the verbal enchantments of Lewis Carroll, James Joyce, and Vladimir Nabokov, those archmagicians of the mother tongue. It was great fun to discover, with Nabokov, that *eros* contains the *sore* and the *rose,* and to unpack a Joycean portmanteau like *penisolate* (on page one of *Finnegans Wake*) with Wellington's Peninsular War and Dublin monument, the late penis, the lonely pen, and Isolde, all neatly folded into one four-syllable satchel. *Dear Aunt Sally, thank you for the red sweater. Dear Aunt Sally, thank you for the red sweater.* Where in my schoolboy experience were the magi of education, the linguists in pointed pun-studded caps who could have given me the power to speak and hear incantations? Children should be taught these things at a Merlin's knee. The banal transcripts of the twentieth century could use a little magic.

◗

From the pass at the top of the Ballyferriter road (*Mam na Gaoithe,* "the Windy Pass"), turn left and skirt the back of the hill behind my house. You are traveling along the Saint's Road, an ancient track that pilgrims once followed from the parish of Ventry northwest to the summit of Brandon Mountain, where Saint Brendan had his hermitage. Some stretches of the medieval track have been tarred or graveled and turned into modern roads; other parts have been plowed and fenced and are now represented on the maps of the Ordinance Survey only as dotted lines. If you follow the solid lines and the dotted lines along the tarred roads or across the fields, you come, about halfway to Brendan's mountain, to the church at Kilmalkedar. A monastic settlement was founded here by Saint Maolcethair in the seventh century (*Kil*, "church"; *malkedar*, "of Maolcethair"), although the present structure dates from the twelfth century. The fine stone building, roofless and weather-worn, is a rare example of early Romanesque architecture in Ireland. The present church almost certainly replaced a prior structure of wood; in certain details of construction (the corner pillars and the "cross-beam" decorations at the apex of the front and rear elevations) there are evocations of the earlier way of building with timber. Some years ago, when I first visited the site, the church yard was overgrown and graves gaped open, exposing a grisly collection of skulls and bones; more recently, the Board of Works has tidied up the place, trimmed the grass, graveled the paths, and sealed the tombs. But no amount of titivation can erase the medieval aspect of Kilmalkedar churchyard. The bones of saints still rattle in the graves, and the hollow-eyed skulls of history peer out from under every stone.

Kilmalkedar is rich in history; it is also a grand physical site, set in a massive frame of rock and sky and open to infinity. The doorless round-arched entrance of the church looks out toward the western end of the Dingle Peninsula, where gently folded strata of Silurian and Devonian sandstones and mudstones have been carved by wind and waves into toothy cliff-girt peaks and sagging sea-filled hollows. In the foreground lies the village of Ballydavid and the silver half-moon of Smerwick Harbour. On the horizon the island of Inishtooskert rises from the floor of the sea like the back of a beached whale. Kilmalkedar was a sacred site even before the coming of the Christian priests. The church yard contains a remarkable assortment of stone artifacts that date from pre-Christian times. One especially fine standing stone is pierced with a sighting hole that is aligned toward the setting of the solstitial sun. When Maolcethair arrived here, with his message of a unitary personal God, he found a people whose religion was rooted in the earth and sky. Against that pagan faith his only weapon was the word.

In the chancel of Kilmalkedar Church there is a stone inscribed with an elegant Christian cross, and along the spine of the stone is carved a Latin alphabet. I trace my finger along the grooves of the letters as a child might have done a thousand years ago to learn the forms of the alphabet—up, down, and around—and each letter is an incantation or a miniature prayer. *In the beginning was the Word*, said the evangelist John. *And the Word was with God, and the Word was God.* With my finger I trace the original prayer: *a, b, c, d.* Abracadabra. With four of those chiseled icons I can make a *rock;* with three, a *sky.* Turn this alphabet-incised stone on its side so that the letters lie flat like the keyboard of a harpsichord; I will sit down in the chancel of Kilmalkedar Church, spread my fingers upon those keys, and play you a universe.

The poet Howard Nemerov says of poetry: "Poetry works on the very surface of the eye, that thin, unyielding wall of liquid between mind and world, where, somehow, mysteriously, the patterns formed by electrical storms assaulting the retina become things and the thought of things and the names of things and the relations supposed between things." Science works there, too, in that thin film on the surface of the eye. The mind and world meet in that layer of liquid and dissolve together. Letters congeal into words, and words into metaphors, and metaphors into sweeping theories. I stand in the doorway of Kilmalkedar Church, and the retina of my eye is swept by electrical storms of images that come rolling off the Atlantic on the back of Icelandic winds, winds that tease up whitecaps in Smerwick Harbour and set the fishing fleet at Ballydavid bobbing like corks. Moisture-laden clouds, driven by an Atlantic low, roll and tumble and nudge against the summit of Mount Eagle like sheep scratching their fleecy backs against a crag. As I watch, what I see and my description of what I see flow together, back and forth, like a river meeting the tide, and the mountains let go of their moorings and they flow too, rising and falling like waves on the sea; the floor of the sea lifts and bends, the face of the cliff crumbles into sand, and the sand is hardened into stone. *Old Red Sandstone, Dingle Beds,* the *Dunquin Group, trilobites, halysites, favosites, brachiopods,* the *Silurian* and *Devonian Periods*—words that I have learned from my geology texts form on my lips, spontaneously, as a kind of poetry or prayer. This is the language of praise.

The church at Kilmalkedar is itself a kind of geology

text. It evolves upward out of its foundations. There are "horizons" in the walls where the mode or the medium of construction was abruptly changed, as if a new architect with new ideas had taken over the job of building, a new abbot, perhaps, for the monastic foundation. At ground level the walls are constructed of a fine violet sandstone, in blocks of almost random shapes, laid in wavering courses; only at the corner pillars are the lowest courses of the walls fashioned with geometrical care. The violet sandstones are part of the Dingle Group of the local sedimentary succession. They were deposited in river beds or shallow lakes about 390 million years ago, at a time when plants from the sea were making the first tentative colonizations of the dry land. (Elsewhere, rocks of the same age contain fossils of the earliest land-dwelling plants.) The violet sandstones rise a fourth of the way up the walls of Kilmalkedar Church, and then the material of construction changes to yellow flagstones streaked with rusty oxides. The flagstones are from the Dunquin Group of the sedimentary succession, and I know from my geology map that they were quarried at the other side of Smerwick Harbour, a distance of five miles from Kilmalkedar. The extra labor of carrying the stones from so far afield was offset by the more regular shape of the stones themselves, which consequently required less working on the site of construction. The rocks of the Dunquin Group were deposited during the Silurian Period of geologic history, about 410 million years ago, in a shallow epicontinental sea. The sediments are fossiliferous and include corals, trilobites, and the shells of brachiopods and gastropods. (I have found these fossils in the cliffs at Smerwick Harbour, but not here in the walls of Kilmalkedar Church, despite careful searching.) There were volcanic islands in the Silurian Sea—the drift of continents was closing up an earlier "Atlantic" ocean—and the corner pillars of the church are fashioned from a soft gray volcanic rock, compacted ash of Silurian age that lent itself to a regular architectural geometry. Halfway up the walls of the church there is yet another material change, this time to gray conglomerates of the Dingle Group, in which pebbles of pink sandstone and quartz are embedded like plums in a pudding. And then again, three-quarters of the way up the walls, the material of constuction becomes a brown mudstone, 350 million years old, quarried from nearby sea cliffs.

The walls of Kilmalkedar Church rise higgledy-piggledy from their foundations, whimsically moving backward and forward in geologic time. Each stone was taken from the body of the Earth, shaped, and put in place. Each stone is a word, each course of stone is a sentence, and the church itself is a volume of praise. I read the walls of the church as I might read a geology text, or a hymnal. They rise paragraph upon paragraph, stanza upon stanza, from the ground, praising. I have on a wall in my house a geological map of Ireland. The colors on the map record a billion years of geologic history; they hint at landscapes never seen; they provide a history for an unseen Earth. The façades of Kilmalkedar Church are like that—multicolored, time-dappled, evocative of unseen terrains.

From Kilmalkedar, the Saint's Road makes straight for the summit of Brandon Mountain, over a ridge, across a valley, and up the western shoulder of the mountain. Brandon is Ireland's fourth-highest peak. From the base of the mountain Saint Brendan the Navigator set out upon the voyage that some say took him to the New World nearly a thousand years before Columbus. On the summit are the ruins of an oratory and a holy well that are associated with the saint. Every year, even to this day, pilgrims follow the Saint's Road to the summit of the mountain. I have often followed that track, from the village of Ballybrack to the summit, in search of Ireland's geological past.

If you want to explore Ireland's past, you must climb its hills. On the flanks of the hills you will find archeological evidence for the island's earliest farmsteads. Higher, on the crests of low hills such as Tara, are the seats of the Celtic kings. And higher yet, on the mist-shrouded summits of the mountains, are megalithic tombs, dolmens, and stone forts that take us back to the myths and legends of Irish prehistory, back even to the moment when Cessair, the granddaughter of Noah, placed the first human foot on Irish soil at Ballinskelligs Bay. And before Cessair, tectonic forces in the Earth were shaping the land that would be Ireland. With instruments of fire and ice, those forces fashioned the quartzite cone of Donegal's Errigal Mountain, the schists and slates of Glendalough, Connemara's green "marble," Kerry's "diamonds," the limestone Rock of Cashel, the polygonal volcanic columns of the Giant's Causeway, the flat-lying sandstone flags of the Cliffs of Moher, the ice-scrubbed shores of the Lakes of Killarney, and the twin glacial drumlins of Armagh, which are today crowned by paired primatial cathedrals, one Roman Catholic, one Church of Ireland. For half a billion years the Earth labored—heaving, folding, cleaving, forging, tempering, and scouring—to perfect the present island. All of this pre-human history can be read from the summits of Ireland's highest peaks.

The earliest chapters of the geological story are written in the twisted loops of purple and brown sandstones that are exposed in the eastern headwall cliffs of Brandon Mountain. Four hundred million years ago, the continents of Europe and North America, drifting across the face of the globe, collided and fused. A range of mountains was pushed up along the suture, of which New England's Appalachians and Donegal's Derryneagh Mountains are the eroded remnants. South of the mountains, in what is now central and southern Ireland—and including the present site of the Dingle Peninsula—there was a low-lying basin. As the mountains eroded, brown and purple sands collected in the basin in horizontal beds. Beneath the weight of these sediments the land subsided, and the sediments thickened further. Then, about three hundred million years ago, the ocean overlapped the land, covering the basin with a shallow inland sea. Thick beds of limestone accumulated on the floor of the sea, burying the sands. These are the limestones that now outcrop all across central Ireland, most dramatically at the Burren in County Clare and at the Rock of Cashel. They also constitute the floor of the Vale of Tralee at the foot of Brandon Mountain.

During the era of the limestone sea, Ireland and Europe lay closer to the equator. The climate was tropical and warm. Sediments continued to accumulate on the floor of the inland sea, and the sea eventually gave way to swamp. Thick layers of vegetative matter were deposited on a limestone base all across Ireland and Britain. Modified by burial and time, these organic materials became the coal that is the basis for Britain's industrial wealth.

But nature was less generous with Ireland. No sooner had Ireland's coal been given than it was taken away. Far away to the south, the drifting continent of Africa pushed against the underside of Europe. That squeeze of continents raised the Alps and gave Ireland a gentle compression that lifted the central lowlands above the level of the sea. Erosion stripped away the newly deposited coal, right down to the limestone. That same thrust from the south folded the rocks of Kerry into parallel ridges. The limestone strata that crowned the ridges was removed by erosion, exposing the underlying sandstones that now form the backbone of the Dingle Peninsula.

Then followed a two-hundred-million-year interval marked by gentle cycles of uplift and subsidence, accompanied by occasional inundations by the sea, but all of this left little effect upon Ireland. What the sea gave by way of depositions, erosion took away. The hiatus ended in an episode of fiery violence. About seventy million years ago the unified continent of Europe and North America split apart along a north–south line, and a new and widening ocean filled the rift. Through faults in the stretched crust, lava welled up to the surface and spread out in thick sheets across the land, forming in the north of Ireland the broad, basaltic Antrim plateau, and—where the volcanic rock came under attack by the sea—the spectacular coastal scenery of that county.

If the penultimate chapter of Irish geological history is a story of fire, the final chapter is a story of ice. Near the summit of Brandon Mountain there are scoured valleys and steep-walled cirques that could have been carved only by glaciers. It was in these mountains that nineteenth-century geologists first recognized the work of the ice in Ireland. Twelve thousand years ago most of the present island lay under a glacial mantle that was part of the great ice sheets that covered much of the northern continents. Few parts of the present surface of Ireland are free of the scrapings or depositions that accompanied the long regime of ice. As the ice sheets advanced and ebbed in repeated pulses of cooling and warming climate, the level of the sea correspondingly fell and rose. At the height of the ice age, the shallow waters that now separate Ireland from Britain and France receded to the deep ocean basin, providing dry passage for animals and plants.

The geological history of Ireland is part of a grander, global story. It is the story of a planet whose eggshell-thin crust rests upon a hot and turbulent interior. It is a story of a planet whose crust has been torn by internal turbulence into rigid sheets—fractured pieces of "eggshell," called plates by geologists—that slip and slide over the molten or semi-molten interior, modifying ocean basins, lifting and deploying continents, squeezing up mountains from the floors of seas, dragging down ocean trenches, triggering episodes of volcanic violence, and changing the patterns of ocean circulation and climate. On a time scale of eons, the Earth has the character of a living organism—vital, animated, transforming. The story of the animated Earth can be read from the summit of Brandon Mountain.

◑

I have heard it said that Eskimos have a dozen words for *snow*, each word corresponding to a different aspect of the Eskimo *experience* of snow. We might approximate any one of the Eskimo snow-words by appending the appropriate adjectives to our word *snow*—"granular, crunchy snow," for example. But presumably that adjectival equivalence does not work quite so immediately on the surface of the eye as does the Eskimo word. Language works best when things and the thoughts of things fit like hand and glove. "A tantivy and tremulous motion of the elm tree tops," wrote Thoreau, and with that one utterly perfect word—*tantivy*—the unyielding wall between mind and world dissolved. The thing and the thought of the thing partook of each other. The elm trees still shake.

Roger Tory Peterson, in the preface to his handbook on wildflowers, lists sixty ways the botanist has for saying that a plant is not smooth: *aculeate, aculeoate, asperous, bristly, brillate, canescent, chaffy, ciliate, cilioate, coriaceous, corrugated, downy, echinate, floccose, flocculent, glandular, glandulisferous, glummaceous, glutinuous, hairy, hispid, hirsutulous,* and so on. Why *aculeate* and *echinate* when *bristly* would seem to serve? Give the botanist his due: His experience of the bristliness of plants is more refined than our own, just as the Eskimo's experience of snow is more refined. The fine distinctions of botanical language reflect the subtlety of the botanical world as it exists on the surface of the botanist's eye.

Distinctions are everything. Rocks are "old," and the stones of Kilmalkedar are "very old." How old? In Kilmalkedar church yard there is a lovely sundial carved onto the face of a standing stone. The dial is marked to tell the five daylight canonical hours—Lauds, Prime, Terce, Sext, and Nones. At the center of the dial is a hole which once received a wooden stick that served as the dial's stylus. I break off the branch of a willow tree and jam it into the hole. The shadow of the stick falls upon the double lines that mark the hour of Terce. So! Across a thousand years this stone serves well enough to mark the hour of the day. And the sundial in Kilmalkedar church yard tells the passage of another kind of time—geologic time. Let me try to read it. The dial is shaped from a slab of coarse gray sandstone, and embedded in the sandstone, like the jewels set into the beaten gold of the Armagh Chalice, there are pebbles of an older purple stone. The purple pebbles were deposited in a river bank with gray sand during Devonian times, 400 million years ago. A few of the purple inclusions are as large as my fist, so the river must have been fast moving to have carried such a load. A closer inspection of some of these larger inclusions reveals that *they* in turn include tiny round pebbles of limestone—pebbles enclosed in pebbles enclosed in pebbles. What does all of this mean? First, the calciferous bodies of a myriad of planktonic creatures accumulated on the floor of an ancient shallow sea, forming beds of calcium carbonate thousands of feet thick. By the agency of pressure and chemical cementation, these sediments were consolidated into limestone. The land shifted, the seafloor rose above the level of the sea, and the limestone was crumpled up into a range of hills. Immediately, erosion began to tear the hills down, bit by bit. That part of the hills that was not dissolved was broken into tiny limestone pebbles that were tumbled along by a river and deposited, with purple silt from another source, in banks at flood stage. Eons passed, the land across which the river flowed subsided, and the river deposits—the purple silts with gray limestone pebbles—were deeply buried beneath further sediments and consolidated. Again, the crust of the Earth buckled, and what had been a deeply buried river valley became a mountain. The purple stone with the included limestone pebbles was broken up by water and weather and tumbled as new pebbles and fist-sized stones by a fast-flowing river into a lowland basin and deposited as pebble bars on the banks of the river. The land subsided, the sea intruded upon the river valley, and the sediments were buried by marine depositions. Now came a squeeze from the south (Africa colliding with Europe) that pushed these newest rocks up, out of the sea, into the backbone of the Dingle Peninsula. Erosion stripped away the overlying strata to reveal at last the gray sandstone with the purple pebbles that contain still older nuggets of limestone. This is the colorful conglomerate that the monks found close by the church at Kilmalkedar a thousand years ago, and from a chunk of it they fashioned the sundial, pecking away at it for weeks, themselves agents of a fresh cycle of erosion; the flakes they chipped from the dial will become part of some future sedimentary stratum.

The sundial tells a story of subsidence, uplift, subsidence, uplift, subsidence, uplift—the crust of the Earth going up and down like an elevator, accepting sediments on the down cycle, shedding them as it rises, in three great cycles of disturbance. If we could speed up the film and make those events that required hundreds of millions of years unfold in minutes, we would see the surface of the Earth convulse like a sea in a storm, heave and collapse, swell and break, and all the while life would be scampering and burrowing and scuttling about, adapting, as best it can, to changing conditions of habitat and climate. It is a huge story, this story that I read in the Kilmalkedar dial, a story of paramount grandeur, and now—*at this instant*—as the shadow of the willow stick falls upon Terce, it also falls upon a limey pebble from Precambrian times, when the only form of life on Earth was microscopic, single-celled, hardly more than a blob of protoplasm encased in a cell wall, but undeniably alive— photosynthesizing, respiring, moving about, possibly re- producing sexually—my ancestor...and, there, I have said it all, told the story of the dial, put it into words.

The monks of Maolcethair's foundation divided the day and night into eight canonical "hours"; the geologist has distinguished the ages of the rocks of the Dingle Peninsula by a score of divisions. First, there are the major periods of the Paleozoic Era, the periods adopted by geologists worldwide, the "canonical" periods of geology—the Silurian, the Devonian, and the Car- boniferous—great blocks of time measured in hundreds of millions of years, reaching from the time of the trilobites to the age of the reptiles. Then, within these extended periods, there are sub-units of geologic time—the Wenlock; the Ludlow; the Downtonian; the Lower, Mid- dle, and Upper Old Red Sandstone; the Tournaaisian; the Visean; and the Namurian—unfolding like successive ticks of the second hand of a clock. As *bristly* can be *aculeate* or *enchinate,* so each of these sub-periods can be further refined: Here, on the Dingle Peninsula, the Old Red Sandstone, for example, is represented—moving forward in time—by the rocks near Eask Tower (green and red sandstones and mudstones), the rocks of the little beach called Trabeg (coarse conglomerates, pebbly sandstones), and the rocks of the cliffs at Ballymore (red and brown sandstones and red shales) and are therefore so named—the Eask Formation, the Trabeg Formation, the Ballymore Formation. But don't be fooled! The crumplings and foldings of the Earth's crust described by these geological terms do not exist back there, somewhere along a time line, independent of ourselves. The Earth's history—*as I have told it*—exists here, now, in that film of liquid on the surface of my eye and at the tip of my tongue. I speak the words—"Eask," "Trabeg," "Ballymore"—and, *abracadabra*, ancient seas flow from the stones, swimming with extinct creatures, conjured into being, with mountains yawning to the sky, rain-worn and pebbly, and I have turned a sundial into time.

In the beginning was the word, and the Word was with God, and the Word was God. All things were made by him and without him was not made any thing that was made. The Roman letters inscribed on the Alphabet Stone in the chancel of the church at Kilmalkedar were introduced into Ireland in the fourth century of the Christian era, although the stone itself is unquestionably of a later date. At about the same time Roman script appeared in Ireland, the Irish were perfecting an alphabet of their own, called ogham, which was popular in the southwest of the country throughout the Dark Ages. The ogham alphabet has survived only as inscriptions on stone, and there is a fine example of such a stone in the church yard at Kilmalkedar. The ogham alphabet consists of slashes beside or across a straight central staff that in practice was usually the sharp edge of a tall standing stone. For example, one stroke orthogonally across the central staff represented *A*; two strokes, *O*; three, *U*; and so on. Half-strokes to one side or the other of the central line, and diagonal strokes across the line, gave the consonants. It was a clumsy alphabet, although easily worked into stone, and it soon gave way to Roman letters, especially for writing onto leather, cloth, or parchment. The ogham inscription at Kilmalkedar reads ANM MAILE-INBIR MACI BROCANN ("The name of Mael-Inbir, son of Brocan"), and a total of seventy-five strokes was required for it to be incised down the spine of the stone.

The western fringe of Ireland is a rubble of stone. The movements of continents over the eons have lifted the Earth's crust again and again to the attack of the elements, to the lick of the incessant wind and tide, which here on the exposed prow of Europe has turned crust into rubble. The church yard at Kilmalkedar and the walls of the church itself contain more kinds of stone, in more curious combinations, than I have seen any-where else in so small a space: stones broken from the face of hills by frost, stones scraped from the mountains by moving ice, stones rolled smooth by moving water,

stones quarried from sea cliffs and tors by medieval monks or Iron Age farmers, stones chipped and chiseled, stones shaped into phalli and crosses, stones carved into the heads of saints and gargoyles, and stones inscribed with two different alphabets, one ogham, one Roman. And, yes, the alphabets are the key, for it is the *word* that turns this rubble of silicates and carbonates into history, into science—into corals growing on Silurian reefs when Europe was bestride the equator; into purple sands dumped into an expanding sea when continents rifted and Europe and North America parted company; into old Mael-Inbir himself, son of Brocan, sword-wielding, cow-butchering Mael-Inbir, alive yet, after fifteen centuries—I can read his name in ogham incisions on stone as clearly as I read "Silurian," "Devonian," and "Carboniferous" in the stone itself—words that come tripping to my tongue in a tantivy of images, from a source here—just here—in that unyielding wall of liquid where image meets reality on the surface of the eye.

SEXT

I Would Be Like a Little Bird

EVEN BEFORE I SEE HIM, I feel the shove of his huge wings. I hear the sound of air moving. I turn, and there he is, flapping up from the foreshore not fifty feet from where I am standing, a gray heron, *ardea cinerea*. I am so close to the bird he is like a part of my own body. I feel the size of him, the huge zeppelin bulk rising into the air, his long legs dangling behind like mooring lines.

Europe's gray heron is a close relative of the great blue heron of North America; to my eye the birds are indistinguishable. In New England, too, I have seen this splendid creature rise from a marsh with a bright fish in his beak, his black-plumed eye gleaming with a fine quartz fire. In certain tribal cultures each person has a totem, an animal or plant that is that person's other self, a creature to which that person's life is inextricably bound by a common ancestry. I am not superstitious; I do not believe in magical links; but if I have a totem, then this great gray bird is it.

The heron circles, across the pier, and then, awkwardly braking with his huge wings, settles on the farther shore. He stands at the edge of the tide on a single cornstalk leg, as still as a reed in unmoving air. He watches for prey, a sand worm or a fish. When a gust of wind from the channel rustles his cope of gray feathers, he shifts his weight to the other foot and adjusts his wings with an episcopal shrug. I watch and wait for the rocket-like extension of the curved neck and the quick stab of the scissors beak.

"You might imagine what you see to be the statue of a bird," wrote John James Audubon of the heron, "so motionless is it. But now, he moves; he has taken a silent step, and with great care he advances; slowly does he raise his head from his shoulders, and now, what a sudden start! His formidable bill has transfixed a perch." Audubon shot the heron. He killed the heron with his gun and propped the lifeless carcass against a tree and painted it. Audubon's painting of the great blue heron is one of his finest; here is the gleaming eye and the cope of heavy feathers—one can even imagine the guttural *quock* emerging from the long, curved throat.

I approach the bird, moving along the foreshore, heron-slow. Tolerantly, he waits. He holds me in the long crook of his eye until he can bear my approach no longer, and then he takes to the air, beating upward, outward, skimming the boats at anchor, circling. I rise with him— totem-follower—all neck and legs, all shoulders and chin. My body is filled up with the bones of him, those hollow bamboo struts that hold his gasbag frame together. I circle with him in the clear air of June, an aureole of bright feathers about our head. For a moment I live with him in that generous skin, in that wrap of gray feathers, afloat on those huge bedsheet wings.

There is something absolute about the way they cleave the air, out there, over the water—the gannets, the cormorants, the kittiwakes, and the guillemots—landless, long-ranging birds, their bright wings lambent in sunlight. A pair of common terns, black-capped and fork-tailed, skim the waters of the channel, small birds that stitch the globe together with their ocean-ranging flights. John Burroughs, the American naturalist ("John-o'-Birds," he was called), wrote that the student of nature has an advantage over people who "gad up and down the world seeking novelty and excitement." The naturalist need only stay at home and watch the procession pass, said Burroughs. And it was true: The great globe swung past Burroughs' cottage door like a revolving showcase, and each change of season was a passage into a strange new land. Nevertheless, here I am, birdwatching far from home, in search of novelty and excitement. What I hope to find on this particular day will on no account come to me.

When at last it is clear that I am the only passenger who will seek transport to the Skelligs, I am beckoned aboard our little boat, and the craft springs smokily to life. For twenty minutes we move down the channel

between Valencia Island and the mainland, bracketed on either side by white cottages and green fields. Then, passing between Bray Head and Black Head, we make for the open sea. Our destination is two small islands that jut from the waters of the Atlantic eight miles off the coast of Kerry. The islands are part of a submerged extension of the rugged Iveragh Peninsula. They stand in eighty meters of water and rise precipitously from the sea. A landing on the larger island, the Great Skellig, is generally feasible only on a fine summer day, and a landing on the Little Skellig is nearly impossible at any time of the year. Often, on a bright, windless day, when one might imagine that a landing would be easy, winds a thousand miles out in the Atlantic Ocean push waves against the islands with a force that would smash a small craft to pieces.

But today the sea is calm, disturbed only by a gentle swell, and the boat's pilot will cover the trouble and expense of my solitary passage with a day of fishing in the rich waters about the islands. There are others out fishing, gannets from the Little Skellig, birds as long as my arm from beak to tail, as streamlined as a sunbeam, snow-white except for the sooty tips of their bladelike wings, cruising a dozen yards above the sea, and falling into the water like a stone—*plunk*—when they sight a fish; the mystery is how a body light enough to float on air can fall with such velocity. (One is reminded of those

experiments with feathers falling in a vacuum that we performed in the high school physics lab.)

As we approach the Little Skellig, a thousand gannets wheel and dive about us like the swirling aftermath of a pillow fight. The island is the second-largest gannetry in the world; it is surpassed in numbers of pairs of nesting birds only by the island of St. Kilda in Scotland's Outer Hebrides. There are 40,000 gannets on the sixteen acres of the Little Skellig. The rock is white with gannets, and in those few places not covered with nesting birds the rock is white with their guano. I have examined the Little Skellig with binoculars from my home, twenty miles away across Dingle Bay; from that distance the island seems to be covered with snow and contrasts sharply with the black double-pyramid of the Great Skellig. In the autumn the gannets move off the Little Skellig to live on the open ocean, and then the island is less white, until the birds return again the following February.

On the Little Skellig there are a lesser number of kittiwakes, guillemots, and razorbills, taking up what space the gannets leave unoccupied on the lower ledges. If there is a cleft on the Little Skellig, there is a bird to fill it; if there is a ledge, it holds a nest. As we cruise close around the island, I have the sense that if all those birds took to the air at once the island would lift with them— one hundred million tons of black sandstone—and fly, westward, oceanward, beyond the other Skellig that now lies dead ahead of the prow of our boat, Skellig Michael, the great one.

●

Great Skellig, that black rock with the lighthouse that blinks nightly at the black sea, is called Skellig Michael, for the Archangel, like those two other famous sea rocks on the coasts of Europe that are dedicated to the Saint. There the resemblance ends. Mount St. Michael in Cornwall and Mont Saint-Michel in Brittany are connected to the mainland by causeways. They are home to substantial communities of permanent residents and are easily accessible to tourists. Ireland's Skellig Michael lies at the end of a sea voyage. Except for the keepers of the light, the island is uninhabited. It is a place of sheer precipices and terrifying landings.

Skellig Michael *was* inhabited throughout the Dark Ages and into medieval times. High on the easternmost peak of the rock, 600 feet above the sea, there are ruins of a monastic settlement, five "beehive" cells and two small oratories constructed of unmortared stone, their corbelled roofs still intact, and walled terraces built into the face of the cliff. The monastery is reached from the sea by a stairway hewn into rock. The ascent is vertical. It is difficult to understand why men chose to live here—or *how* they lived; it is a place fit only for birds. Climatologists believe that Europe's weather was milder in those times than it is today; nonetheless, access to the island by wicker boat would have been infrequent and dangerous. What did the monks eat? Bird eggs and fish are plentiful enough in the spring and summer months, but what of winter? Did the monks grow grain or vegetables on the scanty terraces? Did they maintain goats on the island? On these questions history is silent; there is only an occasional reference to the Skellig in certain of the ancient legends, and a few citations in the Annals of Innisfallen, the Annals of Ulster, and the Annals of the Four Masters, generally recording the sacking of the monastic foundation by Viking raiders. What could Northmen have wanted from this savage rock? How did they gain access? A single man armed with stones could have defended the place against a hundred Vikings.

There is no one on the island to challenge my arrival. The Atlantic is quiet in Blind Man's Cove as we approach the landing, and I have no difficulty jumping from the gunwale of the boat to the security of the little jetty. The boat backs away, and I am left alone. From the cove a narrow road leads to the modern lighthouse at the western end of the island; the road was blasted into nearly vertical rock by nineteenth-century engineers. Halfway along toward the lighthouse I leave the road and climb a stairway that was cut into the living rock a thousand years before the arrival of the engineers. I climb

hand over hand, 400 feet up to the place called Christ's Saddle, a little hammock of greensward slung between two peaks where the slope almost flattens. From here the path turns eastward and ascends another stairway, this one constructed of stone slabs and less precipitous, to the monastic enclosure, 600 steps in all, 600 feet from sea to monastery, like a ladder to an eagle's aerie.

The monastery on the Great Skellig is typical of the eremetical foundations that had their origin in the deserts of Egypt in the earliest centuries of the Christian era and then spread like wildfire over Christian Europe. For a time, every rock and cave from the Red Sea to the coast of Ireland had its saint; every cleft and ledge was a hermitage. Simon of Antioch lived on a pillar in the desert for thirty years. Saint Anthony inhabited a cave with snakes and scorpions as his companions. The Skellig monks built their tiny windowless cells on a shelf of sandstone hardly wide enough to stretch out on. They packed seaweed into chinks in the cliff-face to make a garden. And what did they find on that hard rock? The words of the Psalmist come to mind: *He made darkness his secret place. His pavilion round about him were dark waters and thick clouds of the skies.... And he rode upon a cherub, and did fly: yea, he did fly upon wings of the wind.*

Lord, thou art my rock. A hundred million years ago, continents collided, and the coast of Ireland was crumpled. Sandstone strata deposited in sedimentary basins were tilted almost vertically. Later, the level of the sea rose and drowned the margin of the continent, and what had been hills became islands. From the monastic settlement on Skellig Michael I look back toward Black Head on the Kerry Coast and the tips of the drowned peaks lay all in a line—the Little Skellig, with its cloud cap of wheeling birds, Lemon Rock, and Puffin Island— the submerged hills climb onto the land at Black Head and march all the way to Killarney. In each of the islands there is the same abrupt slant of sandstone angled to the sky. The strata sort themselves out into layers of ocher, black, and brown, like a catalogue of geological eons. The sea about the islands is a clean, hard floor, and the air above is hung like a tent. A tide of description flows back and forth between my ears. *Look, there, how the sandstone strata strike gannetlike against the sea. Listen, there, to the chatter of sea birds and the squeak of the wind. And look, there, where a cloud of kittiwakes follows a shoal of invisible fish.* There is a line in a poem of Seamus Heaney's that quotes Michael McLaverty: "Description is revelation!" *Look, how the light on the sea creates the patterns of moire silk. Listen to the thud of wave against stone.* The act of description is pure and sharp and satisfying, and whatever it is that is sure in this world, whatever it is that is absolute, fixed, and certain, is all about me on the Great Skellig; it lifts, it cleaves, it flattens, it flies on the wings of the wind. Is that what the saints came here to find, that note of revelation? Was that the motive of their exile?

◗

The boat that brought me to Skellig Michael stands far off, in a halo of kittiwakes. Four hours will pass before the boatman returns to retrieve me. There are stories of people put ashore on the Skellig for a day's outing who ended up staying for a month as the uninvited guests of the lighthouse keepers when the weather took a turn for the worse. That is not likely to happen today. The sky shows no hint of storm. I stretch out on a terrace of the monastic enclosure and take a selfish pleasure in the fact that the day is fine and I have the island to myself.

In the grass beside me there are scarlet pimpernels, small five-petaled flowers, not really scarlet but an unusual rose-orange. The sun is at the top of the sky's arch, dead south, at solar noon, and already the blossoms of the pimpernels have closed; on the mainland they will remain open until mid-afternoon. Pimpernels are common along Kerry roadsides and in hedgerows. They have the delicate look of plants that would prefer soft, sheltered spaces—kitchen sills or greenhouse gardens. On the Skellig, they face the full blow of the Atlantic. Not surprisingly they have sought the sheltered hollows of the monastic terraces, hunkering down behind thousand-year-old walls, shunning the exposed precipices outside.

I decide upon a personal census of the island's flora and fauna. I go along the terraces, down to Christ's Saddle, and along the stairs that descend to Blue Cove on the north side of the island. The pickings are slim; there is nothing exotic to be found, nothing that I could not find on the sea cliffs near my house on the mainland across Dingle Bay. The most common Skellig plant is apparently the sea pink, or thrift, with cloverlike flowers and dense tussocks of greenery. They seem to have potted themselves into every chink of the rock. *Armeria maritima* is the Latin name of the plant, and maritime it is, plainly at home on the island, as content on this wild ocean rock as an orchid in a hothouse; the reticent, salt-sniffing blossoms, the swells of green leaves, and the rugged roots are perfectly adapted to life on the exposed cliffs; one can imagine the sea pinks letting go of the cliffs and living entirely at sea, floating on the billows like pink-sailed galleons.

In certain places on the southern slopes of the island, the cover of sea pinks has been infiltrated by rock sea spurry, a plant with tiny pink five-petaled flowers and ferny leaves, less rugged-looking than the pinks, but equally well adapted to the island. I have read that the rock sea spurry is thriving on the Skellig and may eventually displace the sea pinks altogether. And I find stone crop, sea campion, pearlwort, and scurvy grass—the Viking colonizers of the North Atlantic—compact, muscular, leathery plants, ascetic and salt-tolerant; give these plants a crag and a grip and they will make themselves at home. I have read something else about the Skellig plants. Many of them have established a relationship with a particular species of bird. Sea spurry thrives near the burrows of the puffins. Lower on the cliffs, mayweed and sorrel cohabit with gulls. Orache and scurvy-grass share ledges with nesting fulmars. Whether there is a subtle chemical alliance between the plants and the birds, or whether pairs of cohabiting species find the same island niches to their common taste, is a matter that (as far as I know) has not been resolved by botanists and ornithologists.

The birds and plants of Skellig Michael have estab-

lished a refined pattern of settlement, a quieter, more dignified way of life than what we saw on the Little Skellig. On the larger island there are none of the raucous chattering masses of competing species, none of the ubiquitous whitewash of excrement. And no gannets to overwhelm the island by sheer numbers; those great goosey creatures have seen fit to leave the larger Skellig alone. On Skellig Michael there *are* gulls, razorbills, kittiwakes, fulmars, guillemots, and manx shearwaters in the hundreds or thousands, but their presence is unobtrusive. The island is presided over by the aristo-cratic puffin, the tourist's favorite, a gawky, big-headed, ambling sort of bird, in a penguin's black-and-white tuxedo, but with a bill that looks as if it were dipped into a child's paint pots—primary red, blue, and yellow. The puffins make their nests in the burrows of rabbits (after first rudely tossing out the legitimate residents), and in each nest the female lays a single egg. They fish during the day in the waters near the island. Puffins are great swimmers and divers; they go deep and use their wings as efficiently under water as in the air; human divers have seen puffins fifteen meters below the surface of the sea, flapping about in search of fish.

The puffin presides, but the bird that populates Skellig Michael in the greatest number is the storm petrel. During my afternoon on the island I have not seen a single member of the species, but I know they are here, well hidden, and in the evening, when I am gone, they will emerge from their hiding places, like bats from a dark cave, to frolic about the island, close above the sea, their tiny webbed feet dangling so low that they will appear to be running upon the water.

One night last summer as I lay awake listening to a gale rage about the house, I heard a *thump*, and I knew that something windblown had arrived from the sea. In the morning I found it, a storm petrel, in the garden where it had fallen. I lifted the little corpse and held it in my hand; it had a surprising lightness, as if it were made of papier-mâché. The fully grown adult bird fit neatly into the cup of my palm, and this was a bird quite capable of spending half a year on the open ocean without touching land. From the tip of his tiny beak to the end of his square tail, he was no more than six inches long. The sooty, white-rumped carcass showed no sign of injury from the impact with the wall of my house.

Storm petrels do not usually fly inland, not even for the mile or so that separates the house from the sea. The bird I held in my hand was probably off course, out of control, perhaps utterly exhausted and carried pell-mell by the wind as if he were a tuft of thistle. How does so slight a creature, no larger than a sparrow, survive the winter months, October to April, on the storm-churned North Atlantic? His protection must be his very slightness. He is an invisible mote in the eye of the wind; he cakewalks the wildest wave on tiny webbed feet and bobs on the billows as freely as a cork.

Some biologists maintain that birds are of the same race as the dinosaurs, and that the resilience of my petrel is evolution come full circle. Sixty-three million years ago a great cosmic catastrophe, possibly the impact of an asteroid or comet swarm with the Earth, brought an end to the age of dinosaurs. Triceratops and tyrannosaurus rex, the thunder-footed sovereigns of their race, were toppled, with all others of their kind, in one of the planet's most calamitous episodes of mass extinction. But (say these biologists) the dinosaurs are *not* extinct; they are all about us in disguise, beating the air with that most remarkable of dinosaur inventions, the feather. The first animals with feathers were small dinosaurs of the Jurassic Era, called archaeopteryx. These plumed aviators had mastered flight by the time of crisis when triceratops and tyrannosaurus rex became extinct. When the catastrophe came, the feathered dinosaurs survived to become the modern birds, and the secret of their survival is the storm petrel's secret—go with the flow, ride the wind, hide in the eye of the storm.

So what happened to the bird that came rocketing out of the storm, to end a sixty-three-million-year journey against the wall of my house? He stepped too high above the waves, perhaps, and was carried away by the gale. Or *maybe* he was on course, after all, doing what he intended to do, shrewdly riding the wind, and the house just happened to get in the way. If the house had not been there, then the wind would have carried him up and over the hill, across the backbone of the peninsula, and down again to the sea; and when the storm subsided, he would have been halfway to the Faeroes, or Iceland, or the New World, or wherever it was he was heading, safe and sound, and a ride of a thousand miles in the course of the night would have been nothing to this bird that uses the Atlantic as his birdbath. The house had no business being there; for a million years the hillside had been unobstructed, and then—*thump*—the house popped up overnight, and a philosophy of life that had survived the impact of asteroids developed an unexpected hitch.

The settlement on Skellig Michael—that cluster of monks' cells perched on a crag—was sacked by Vikings in A.D. 795 and again in 812. In 823 the Northmen came once more and this time carried away Eitgal, the Abbot of Skellig, and subjected him to death by starvation. When Turgesius, King of the Danes, swept the Irish coast in 833 and 839, pillaging from sleek clinker-built longboats, the Skellig community was sacked again. Why? What could the Northmen have sought here? A few holy vessels, perhaps, hardly worth the bother. Or was it the challenge of the thing, an unwillingness to admit that it could not be done, the pride of the clean sweep, the same absolutism of motive that brought the monks to the island in the first place, the same motive that lured me to the island across seven miles of sea. It cannot be denied: There is a stubborn quiddity about the place that is irresistibly attractive.

In the face of the Viking attacks—or because of them (that stubbornness again!)—the community survived. Legend has it that the Viking Olav Trygvasson, who was later to become King of Norway and father of that nation's patron saint, was baptized by a Skellig monk, and that his conversion brought an end to the episodes of sack

and pillage. References to the Skellig are sparse in medieval literature, but some sort of occupancy of the island seems to have persisted until the fourteenth century. Then several hundred years of silence pass before the island is mentioned again, this time as a place of pilgrimage and penance. In the eighteenth century, pilgrims from all over Europe came to the rock at Eastertide. Following rock-carved Stations of the Cross, they made the difficult 700-foot climb from sea-level to the Needle's Eye, the precipitous westernmost pinnacle of the island. The culmination of the ordeal required the penitent to crawl out upon a horizontal slab of rock that projects with a dizzy precariousness from the topmost summit and there kiss a stone cross affixed to the end of the slab. The projecting slab and the stone cross are still in place, and I make my way to them. The ascent from Christ's Saddle to the Needle's Eye is terrifying. Hand- and footholds have been cut into the face of the peak, and these one must negotiate, with nothing below but wheeling birds and crashing breakers. I inch my way along, keeping my back flat against the rock, and my legs shake like the tines of a tuning fork. At the top of the pinnacle I creep out to that ultimate station, my arms and legs clasped talonlike about the projecting slab. I press my nose against the cold stone and hold on for dear life. In that moment of crazy accomplishment, every shred of my mainland self is gone and I am a simple thing, like a limpet on a surf-scrubbed stone or a kittiwake on the wing, a thing of tissue, scale, and feather, pure adrenalating flesh, uncomplicated by passion or consciousness, sanctified by fear.

Philosophers of the Middle Ages, following the Greeks, believed that the terrestrial world was fabricated of four elements—earth, air, water, and fire—although these seldom existed, if ever, in an unmixed state. It strikes me, as I cling trembling to this spit of stone, a kind of primitive, inchoate, self-justifying thought, hardly a thought even, more like a desparate image flashed onto the brain's blank screen, that the Greeks and the Scholastic philosophers were right, the world is a vessel of four elements, and here, on the Skellig (as once before on Mount Eagle across the bay), the elements have been winnowed one from another—rock, wave, sky, sun—all pure and disentangled, except for one knot, my shivering self, a knot that ties the threads of the pure elements together, a vinculum, a nexus, like the exquisite ligature that ties a wasp's head to its body, and if I let go my paralyzed grip on my dizzy perch, the threads of the elements will unravel and the whole tapestry of creation will fall into pieces.

Four o'clock. It is the arranged time for my return to the mainland. I make my way to Blind Man's Cove, but the boat isn't there. The sea is calm and the wind is low; it cannot be on account of the weather that I have been abandoned. I walk back up along the lighthouse road to a place with a better view of the sea. Nothing! There are birds, of course, everywhere, fishing, and the bobbing head of a seal, but no boat. Anxiously, I climb back to Christ's Saddle, where the view to the north and south is unobstructed. The sea is empty. I check my watch. Has there been a mix-up on the time?

I return to the cove. The seal that I had seen from the road has moved nearer and now seems to be watching me with as much curiosity as I am watching the empty sea. The seal's big black eyes are almost human. The humped nose that floats on the swell identifies him as a gray seal; probably like me he is a temporary visitor to the island. If I am stuck on the Skellig, the seal will be a mute, but sympathetic, companion. But how long would I last here without human company? Grant, for a moment, the satisfaction of my material needs; grant, even, a modicum of comforts—a cottage, say, such as the lighthouse keepers have, rather than the cold, dark cells of the monastic enclosure; then, in the face of my aloneness, could I summon the courage to endure, as the monks endured? My life has not been without solitude. On walks of discovery I prefer to be alone, so that the voice of description can proceed undistracted—that voice of the internal tour guide. *Look, there is a gray seal, watching, with coal-black eyes and a humped nose. Look, the sea is otherwise empty and shines like bottle-glass.* But what if I were required to spend days, weeks, or even years alone on the Skellig Rock, with the mental dialogue of description running continuously, like an endless tape, the archive between the ears filling to bursting—*look, look, look, look*—even in the dark night the machinery of the brain grinding away like the mechanism of the lighthouse, casting its beam of consideration into every murky mile of the sea—*look, look, look, look*—until the time came when...what?

For a thousand years hermits sat on the Skellig rock and searched the sea for some sign of the Absolute, as on other rocks all across Europe, North Africa, and the Near East they probed the desert, sea, and sky for the signature of God. The eremetical movement was not unique to early and medieval Christianity; every religious tradition has had its hermits, as every time and place has thrown

up men and women who have sought a dangerous solitude. But during the centuries when the Skellig flour-
ished as a place of hermitage, the eremetical movement
was like a frenzy. Young men ran away to solitude as later
they would run away to the sea, and young women shut
themselves up in convents for the love of God. What did
they find?

Listen to one of their own: Richard Rolle was born in
Yorkshire at the beginning of the fourteenth century into
a family of modest, but comfortable means. At the age of
fourteen he was sent up to Oxford, a sophisticated,
stimulating, cosmopolitan place, a hub of learning and
disputation. Rolle was not happy. Metaphysics seemed
empty and remote from real experience; the knowledge
he committed to memory at the university seemed to
lack the immediacy of direct experience. Before the end
of his course of study he gave it up and, at the age of
eighteen or nineteen, returned to Yorkshire. He fashioned
himself a dress of rough cloth (a self-consciously her-
mitlike dress) and set out across the moors. The rest of
his life was spent in solitude and contemplation. "What is
God?" asks Richard Rolle; "I say that you shall never
have an answer to this question. I have not known; angels
know not; archangels have not heard. Wherefore how
would you know what is unknown and also unteach-
able?" This sort of thing did not go down well at Oxford,
where scholars spent their waking hours posing and
refining definitions of God. God, says Rolle, is unknowable. Yet Rolle spent all his life seeking a perfect knowledge of God. He was not bothered by the paradox that
what is unknowable might also be known. The result of
his spiritual exercises—solitude, self-mortification,
prayer, and auto-hypnotic fixation on the name of Jesus—

was what one might call a "mystical experience," a fierce physical *heat* in his breast, an all-enveloping honeylike *sweetness*, and *song*, a pure ethereal music that he heard both outside and within.

It would make little sense to press Rolle too closely as to the actual nature of these experiences. Were they the product of an overly fervid imagination? Were they delusions induced by fatigue, poor diet, and mortification of the flesh? Were they the madness of the endlessly unreeling tapes of solitude gone haywire, spinning off the reels into a hallucinatory tangle? Or—whatever the nature of the experience or its cause—did Rolle find in solitude a kind of pure knowledge, a participation in what simply *is*, a storm petrel's kind of knowledge ("I would be like a little bird," says Rolle), wind, wave, endlessly rocking, a knowledge that—as Rolle insists—has its source not in speculation but in love and intuition? "He warms me and makes me fat," says Rolle, "and all the leanness of longing is put away."

All of this is undeniably attractive. But there is something missing from Richard Rolle's mysticism, something I am not prepared to do without. Rolle put off the things of this world, and the knowledge of those things, to live within that "cloud of unknowing" that was touted by another great mystic of his century. He wished to be ravished by "things unseen." But I am a scientist. If I am to encounter God, it must be as the ground for "things seen." If I am to encounter mystery, it must be within the interstices of "things known." It is something of that engagement with "things seen" and "things known" that I have sensed on Skellig Michael. The Skellig monks could not flee entirely into themselves. The Atlantic pressed them; the rock lifted them. They did not live in a "cloud of unknowing," but in a very real Atlantic mist. Their heat was in the sun and their sweetness in the hive. They clamped their anchorage to the rock and listened to the song of the wind. They colonized the Skellig crag like the sea pinks and stole their burrows like puffins. And, if I am right, they found the Absolute in the elements and took their pleasure and their knowledge from *things seen.*

◗

The Great Skellig has an area of forty-four acres, or that is its cross-section at sea level. At least forty-three of those acres are too steep for human habitation. The lighthouse on the western, oceanward side of the island is built on a ledge blasted from the cliff. The medieval monastery is on one of the few relatively flat natural platforms, but walls and backfill were necessary to create livable terraces. At no time could the little cluster of cells have comfortably sheltered more than a dozen monks. Of the many monastic communities on the wilder coasts of Europe, this must have been considered the most inhospitable—the Ultima Thule of the spirit. But the island did not languish for human inhabitants; a viable community endured here for almost a thousand years.

But at last the eremetical fire spent itself, and the rock reverted to the birds. A cooling climate in the early Middle Ages may have made life on the Skellig intolerable for all but the most devout anchorites. Meanwhile, all across Europe the building of national economies was accompanied by a growing secularism. The dark, shadowy oratories of the island hermits gave way to the grandiloquent visual poems of the urban cathedrals. At the end of the twelfth century, Giraldus Cambrensis, a

Welsh historian, reported that the Skellig monks had moved to the mainland, to a place called Ballinskelligs.

With a seal and puffins for my companions, I wait at Blind Man's Cove, and at last my ferry to the mainland comes chugging into view from behind a shoulder of the island, to take out one last pilgrim—a tourist, really, testing the mettle of his spirit against the hard reality of this spare and beautiful place. As I jump from the jetty onto the boat, the seal backs off and nods. A puffin winks. They knew I would not last.

And perhaps it is just as well. A hundred million years of evolution insist that the Skellig rock belongs to the birds. Humans never had any business here. The rock is not a place for the meddlesome interior voice, for the hankering heart, for heat, for sweetness, or for song. Better that the rock is scrubbed clean of metaphysics, to become again a stark bone of sandstone jutting from the sea, with only the birds to parse and decline.

And now, as I recall the history of that ocean crag and the ways in which humans have used and abused it, I am reminded of one of the puffin's unfortunate cousins, the great auk, or gairfowl. The great auk is a tall, ungainly bird that much resembles the razorbill, but with stumpy, useless wings like a penguin's. It once inhabited the islands of the North Atlantic in huge numbers, and it is now extinct. Monks on the Skellig gathered the eggs and ate the flesh of the great auk; that the bird was for centuries an important source of food is evidenced by the quantities of bones found in kitchen middens at many now-abandoned Irish coastal settlements. The bird was a powerful diver and swimmer, and, although generally helpless on land, it was undoubtedly an elusive and resourceful predator in its own element. Until a few centuries ago, great auks were numerous on both sides of the Atlantic. Richard Hakluyt describes in his *Voyages* the appalling slaughter of great flocks of auks at the hands of early explorers. The encounter of humans with the auk was one-sided from the start. The great auk had the misfortune of being almost totally useful—eggs and flesh were delicious, the feathers made excellent bedding, the carcass was rich with oil. Throughout the eighteenth century the decimation of auk colonies continued apace. The last great auk in Ireland was captured in Waterford Harbour in May 1834. A fisherman netted the bird, exhausted and half-starved, as it begged for food. The lonely creature, the last of its race, lived on in captivity for several months on a diet of fish and mashed potatoes.

NONES

A Thousand Years
in Your Sight

ALONG THE WESTERNMOST SHORE of the Dingle Peninsula, between Clougher Head and Sybil Head, the sea has
notched the cliffs with a maze of caves and coves.
Descent into many of these sea-nibbled recesses is difficult or impossible, but the reward can be worth the risk.
At low tide the rocks on the exposed shingle contain the
peninsula's richest trove of fossils. One place where
access to the sea's edge is relatively easy and the fossils
are plentiful is at Ferriter's Cove, below Sybil Head. The
strata exposed in the cliffs at the cove abound with
geological puzzles. For more than a century, geologists
have come here to ponder the peculiar and unresolved
intricacies of the geology of the Dingle Peninsula.

I have on my desk a reproduction of a watercolor
sketch of James Flanagan, fossil collector with the Geological Survey of Ireland, made at Ferriter's Cove on
September 9, 1856, by his colleague George Victor Du
Noyer, also of the Survey. Flanagan is attired in the
country tweeds that were the standard uniform of field

geologists at that time, heavy, uncomfortable clothes that must have been extraordinarily burdensome when wet. He carries the tools of the geological collector: hammer, compass, leather satchel, notebook, pen, inkpot, and pipe. The stem of Flanagan's clay pipe is broken—the fatality, perhaps, of a scramble down a rough slope to the sea's edge. And Flanagan's jacket appears to have been hastily patched at the elbow—another badge of the field collector.

Physically, the coast of Ireland at Ferriter's Cove has changed little in the hundred years since Du Noyer took time out from research to make his portrait of Flanagan. The sea still throws itself in great heaps upon the land's edge, stirring the shingle with a gravelly roar. Sybil Head still falls into the cove along the same vertical stratum of glistening sandstone. The volcanic crag at Clougher still towers above folded and faulted sedimentary formations. And with a little scratching about on the face of the cliffs, I find samples of the same marine fossils of the Silurian Period that posed the question that perplexed several generations of Irish geologists: Are the rocks of the entire peninsula of a Silurian age, or is this cove of fossiliferous stone oddly out of place, like an extra piece of a jigsaw puzzle that has somehow found its way into the wrong box?

One hundred years ago there was hardly a wilder place in all of Ireland for human habitation than this westernmost tip of the Dingle Peninsula. The standard of life was exceedingly poor. The countryside was often gripped by famine. The life of a field geologist in such an environment could not have been easy. Comfortable accommodation west of Dingle Town was probably difficult if not impossible to find. The geologists' workday began at 9:00 A.M., six days a week. First came the ten-mile walk from Dingle to the cliffs with the puzzling fossils, then hours of field work and mapping, more likely than not in mist or rain. The workday ceased in time to allow the researchers to return to their base of operations by 6:00 P.M. In the evening, around the hearth in a Dingle public house, wet tweeds steaming in the heat of the fire, the geologists transferred their observations to the huge paper base maps that were a growing portrait of the island's geological past. Today, the human environment is rather different at Ferriter's Cove. Tourists fish and swim along the broken shore. There is a comfortable modern hotel only a stone's throw from the fossiliferous strata. There is a golf course atop the enigmatic Silurian beds.

James Flanagan and George Victor Du Noyer were two of "Jukes' men." Joseph Beete Jukes was director of the Irish Geological Survey. He came to Ireland in 1850 after several very happy years with the Geological Survey in England and Wales. It was not a move that he made with pleasure. For Jukes, the Irish directorship meant exile in a primitive place. What drew him to Ireland was *scale.* The geological mapping of Ireland was proceeding on base maps drawn to a scale of six inches to the mile. In the rest of Britain, the scale of geological cartography was one inch to the mile. It was the possibility of greater exactitude offered by the six-inch maps that attracted Jukes. He was a man who was meticulous in attention to detail.

The exact observation of nature and close attention to detail were habits that were widely cultivated in England at the time when Jukes went off to Cambridge for his higher education. Like other aspiring young naturalists among his classmates, Jukes spent more time in the countryside than in the library. The rocks, flora, and fauna of Cambridgeshire were more willingly courted than the classical authors of Greece and Rome. During one of his geologizing walks Jukes might have encountered Charles Darwin, who also haunted the fields and byways on expeditions of discovery. Both Jukes and Darwin were protegés of the geologist Adam Sedgwick, then a professor at Cambridge. It was Sedgwick who inspired Jukes to pursue a career in geology.

After taking his degree, Jukes spent a few years tramping about England, collecting rocks and fossils, and delivering lectures on geology to anyone who would listen. Then, like Darwin, he went off for several years of adventure and observation in remote parts of the world. He was geological surveyor to the colony of Newfoundland. He visited Australia, the East Indies, and the islands of the Pacific. Upon his return to England, there followed three years of geological work in England and Wales. Then, in 1849, came marriage, and the opportunity to map the rocks of Ireland.

Joseph Beete Jukes was director of the Geological Survey of Ireland for twenty years. Those years have been called "the golden age of Irish geology." Jukes and his men explored every corner of the island. They climbed every mountain crag and scrambled down every seaside cliff. They had themselves ferried to wild western islands. They left—literally—no stone unturned. They were guided by a paramount tenet of the science of their time—that by the *sheer bulk* of their observations, classifications, catalogues, and maps, they would ultimately reveal nature's deepest secrets.

My father shared that faith in the force of accumulated data. He was in that sense a scientist in the tradition of Darwin and Jukes. He had no formal training in the sciences. He worked all of his life as an engineer or a teacher. But he maintained that science is a frame of mind. Science, he said, is another name for curiosity. It is the search for patterns of order where chaos apparently reigns. It is the business of compiling data and looking for correlations. All of his life my father drew graphs, with colored pencils on paper with grids of tiny squares, in his meticulous hand. He graphed the family's finances. He graphed the course of national events. He graphed the weather. He graphed sunspot cycles. He graphed the performance of his students. And, as he lay dying from cancer, he graphed the terrible course of his disease.

The nature of the data that occupied my father on his sickbed was various. He asked for instruments, and we supplied them. He wanted a six-inch rule, a meter stick, a protractor, a clock, and a calendar. He wanted notebooks. Hourly he measured his position on the bed and the angles of his limbs. He timed the cycles of pain and medication. He carefully recorded the slow progrcss of the disease as it crept through his body—beginning at the groin, tunneling through the marrow of the bones, finally reaching every extremity. He was not inattentive to things that others would have considered irrelevant. He noted alterations of light and shadow. He followed the phases of the moon. He asked for a barometer so that he could monitor the pressure of the air. This huge mass of numbers he entered into his notebooks with a script that decayed from the draftsmanlike lettering of an engineer to the almost indecipherable scrawl of a victim wasted by cancer. He was convinced that if only he took enough data the cure for his disease would manifest itself, or, if it did not, that his observations would be of value to others who suffered the same affliction.

He would beat "this thing," he said, and he meant it. And so he listened intently for the electrical static of pain that crackled through his wounded nerves, synapse by synapse. He insisted that he felt better if his head was exactly four centimeters from the top of the bed, so all night we measured, and when the pain walked his body down the sheet we jacked him back up. It was "just a matter of science," and the confidence in his voice would have nudged a comet into a new orbit. Confidence is the absolute and only prerequisite of honest research, he said. His calculations and graphs predicted tides of comfort and pain, the ebb and flow of energy in his veins. The cycle is the curve of life, he said, the curve of hope. And no one was more surprised than he when the poison at last reached his tongue and proved every graph and calculation wrong.

I cannot think of my father without the image of graph paper coming into mind—crisp, thin paper, as crinkly as cellophane, printed with precision grids of orange or green lines. There was something about the eternal regularity of those tiny squares repeating them-selves over and over, as if they had no beginning and no end, that was like his vision of the universe itself. The graphs he drew in colored pencils on those sheets seemed to emerge from the paper like the trajectories of particles following fundamental laws of force, tracing the fixity of existence. Behind the apparent chaos of events he recog-nized a geometrical order. My father had taught high school geometry in the years immediately preceding his death. His final project, conceived in the last weeks of his life, was a textbook entitled *Plane Geometry for Anyone.* The manuscript began with the definition of a "point." It went no further. His body had a point to make, and it was final.

I have the journals that my father kept on his sickbed—five volumes that record the melancholy events of his last twelve weeks. The journals constitute the most complete record of a dying that I have ever seen. But he would not have called them that—"the record of a dying." They were research notebooks. They were data. Everything was recorded, for he was convinced that if a cure for his disease were to be found it would be where no one had looked before. The key to a cure might be as simple as a single sensation, but only if that sensation could be placed into a context of line and number. He invented a symbolic calculus of his disease. Each medication, each part of his body, each muscular movement was assigned an abbreviated notation, so that after a while the journals began to take on the appearance of a code. Each variable in his condition was quantified. On almost every page of the journals there is a diagram of his body, as fully and carefully annotated as an architect's plan. The margins are jammed with numbers—inches, milligrams, slopes, percentages, angles.

And from this mass of numbers, patterns began to emerge, the most important of which was a cycle of pain and well-being to which all else was keyed. From the consideration of this cycle he evolved a theory in which pain is not so much a pathological encumbrance as a revealed presence, like the muddy floor of a lake from which the water has been drained. In his theory, pain is something that is always present, even in the healthy body, but hidden by a positive "energy." The effect of his medications, he believed, was not to "kill pain," but to regenerate the overlying strata of energy. To restore him to health, those strata had to be put into place with the exactness of a bricklayer building an arch. Inevitably, this led to certain disagreements with his doctors and the staff of the hospital about how and when medications should be administered. He was persistent in his requests, but not adamant. He was always a little surprised that the doctors and nurses did not immediately grasp the significance of his discoveries. He was discouraged by what he thought was the singlemindedness of the medical profession.

In the end his own theories hardened into a new orthodoxy. What had been a quest became a palliative. What had been honest research became a prop. The flow of space and number in his journals became a grid as rigid as any on a piece of graph paper. Curiosity became complaint. The four centimeters between his head and the top of the bed emerged as a tyrannical absolute. The temperature of the room, the angle of the light, the width of the crack at the door were not allowed to vary by a jot. It is easy to forgive him that singleness of purpose. Constancy is the last line of defense in the face of the inevitability of death. The endlessly repeating graph of his "cycle," carefully maintained in his notebooks until the day of his death, was a line that Death would dare not cross.

The problem of the age of the "Dingle Beds" exercised Irish geologists for almost a century. It was a problem that Joseph Beetes Jukes inherited from Richard Griffith, the first important cartographer of the Irish rocks. It was the fossils from the cliffs at Ferriter's Cove that posed the problem. In 1839 those fossils had been collected by Griffith and sent off to London to be examined by the foremost paleontologists of the time. The verdict came back—the fossils were of Silurian age. Farther east, nearer to the limestone Vale of Tralee, the rocks of the Dingle Peninsula were quite clearly part of the Old Red Sandstone succession, from what we now call the Devonian Period, and fifty million years younger than the Silurian. What then of the strata between? Were they Silurian or Devonian? The question might now seem of little consequence, but the problem was momentous at the time, and for reasons that were personal and social as well as scientific.

The geological battle of Ferriter's Cove was a backwater skirmish in a larger war, a war of ideas and personalities that involved, in one way or another, many of the leading geologists of the early nineteenth century. The chief antagonists were, on the one hand, Henry De la Beche, the first director of the Geological Survey of Britain, and, on the other, Roderick Murchison and Adam Sedgwick of the Geological Society of London. At issue was the proper interpretation of those formations that (as we now know) were laid down between three hundred and four hundred million years ago. There was more involved in the controversy than theoretical geology; careers and reputations turned upon the outcome of each skirmish in the war. The status and prestige of scientific institutions waxed and waned with the rise and fall of hypotheses. Egos swelled and shrank with each new coloring of the geologic maps. This war of ideas has been called "the Great Devonian Controversy." The war was essentially over in 1856 when Murchison himself came to

Ferriter's Cove (he was now director of the British Geological Survey and successor to De la Beche). In the company of Jukes, Du Noyer, and the seventy-one-year-old Griffith, Murchison spent six days examining the geology of the Dingle Peninsula. The little group arrived at a tentative consensus: Excepting the undoubted Silurian strata near Ferriter's Cove, the Dingle rocks should be assigned to the Old Red Sandstones of the Devonian. It was a decision that would be vigorously challenged by the next director of the Irish Survey.

There were other things on Murchison's mind besides rocks. The weather was foul. He was offended by the Roman Catholicism of the Irish. He found the food and the accommodations deplorable. "Catch me going to Ireland again," he is said to have complained. But Murchison was impressed by the robustness of the field workers of the Irish Geological Survey. They endured, he noted, conditions that no self-respecting Englishman would tolerate. In England especially, professional geologists were trapped in a socially embarrassing situation. The nature of their work required them to spend time outdoors, in rough terrain and in all kinds of weather, "breaking rocks." They often found that they were not accorded the gentlemanly status that their sense of personal advancement required. To distinguish themselves from ramblers and rock-breakers of a lower class, the geologists went about their work in formal dress, which often included even a top hat. In his seventies, Richard Griffith could be found ranging the Dingle mountains dressed in a swallow-tail coat and top hat, in pouring rain, hammer in hand. A weatherproof slicker might have been more appropriate dress, but the exigencies of field work took second place to the emblems of station and rank.

On several occasions I have met young geologists down from Dublin or Belfast at work on the cliffs near Ferriter's Cove. They are invariably dressed in sturdy boots and jeans and anoraks, and they are unconcerned with questions of class. Nor does the question of the assignment of the Dingle Beds to the Devonian or Silurian systems any longer excite them. New controversies exercise their curiosity. There are larger tectonic questions in the wind now—questions regarding the closing and opening of the Atlantic Basin, continent-shaping events that took place as the sedimentary formations of the Dingle Peninsula were being laid down. But the young contemporary geologists share a continuity of purpose with the researchers who investigated the rocks of Ferriter's Cove more than a century ago—they share a common search for patterns of order, patterns of a greater scope than those that describe *this particular place* and *this particular time*. Like Jukes, Du Noyer, Griffith, and Murchinson, the geologists in jeans and anoraks are looking for the *universal law* that lies hidden in the broken and tumbled strata of the cove.

The Silurian formations at Ferriter's Cove are indeed an anomaly—a puzzle piece in the wrong box. We now know that the other rocks of the Dingle Peninsula are of the Devonian Period, fifty million years younger. All of the rocks of the peninsula—Silurian and Devonian—date from a time when continents were vigorously on the move, riding the mobile plates of the Earth's crust. While the sedimentary strata of the peninsula were being laid down, North America was pivoting on the equator and drifting slowly northward. Europe was moving north and west toward America. What is now Asia was then a flotilla of unattached mini-continents gliding eastward. Australia, Antarctica, Africa, and South America were united in a single supercontinent that was sliding up from the south. Between 430 million and 300 million years ago these rafts of continental rock collided to form the unified land mass that geologists call Pangaea ("all-earth"). Mountains were lifted along the sutures. In the force of the collisions the earth quaked. Volcanoes erupted. Horizontal strata were tilted vertically. Beds of rock were broken, bent, and overturned. The puzzle pieces were mixed and scrambled. Jukes and his colleagues knew nothing of this. The idea that the continents move laterally on the face of the Earth would have been incomprehensible to them. The notion that the rocks at Ferriter's Cove and the rocks of Newfoundland were once contiguous—neighboring "counties" of Pangaea—would have challenged their credulity. Jukes had worked in Newfoundland. Two thousand miles of ocean now separate Newfoundland from Ireland. It did not occur to Jukes that there was a time when he could have walked from Dingle to Newfoundland in as little time as he presently made the journey from Dublin to Dingle.

The watery ocean was the red herring of nineteenth-century geology. From the cliffs at Ferriter's Cove the ocean has a fixed and permanent look. Rocks crumble in the face of it. Mountains rise and fall; the ocean endures. Or so it seemed to Jukes and his contemporaries. Today we know that the ocean basins are geologically quite distinct from the water that fills them. The water on the Earth's surface endures, but the basins that contain it are ephemeral. The water hides what is really important. Remove the water that thinly covers three-quarters of the globe, and the secret of the crust is starkly revealed. Down the middle of the ocean basins there is a linear range of mountains higher than Brandon Mountain and tens of thousands of miles long. The mountains are the ragged wound where the Earth's crust is being lifted from below and torn apart. Along the spine of the range there is a deep valley—the mid-ocean rift—floored with fresh volcanic rock. If Jukes could have walked along the floor of the mid-Atlantic rift—a valley steaming with volcanic vapors and oozing lava—he would have recognized soon enough the lateral movement of the Earth's crust. If he had climbed the steep escarpments at the sides of the rift and walked down the flanks of the mid-ocean ridge, he would have quickly discovered that the rocks are older the farther he moved from the rift. If he had walked a thousand miles along the floor of the Atlantic Basin, away from the mid-ocean ridge, until he reached the continental slope at Newfoundland or Ireland, he would have found that the rocks of the ocean floor are nowhere more than several hundred million years old. The ocean floors are geologically young. They have been extruded at the rift—oozed up from below—as the Atlantic Basin widens. The entire Atlantic Basin is younger than the youngest rocks at Ferriter's Cove!

So, the secret of drifting continents was there all the time on the floor of the sea, hidden by waters three miles deep, and all of the tramping and hammering and scribbling and collecting by Jukes and his men *on land* could never have revealed the secret of the depths. Puzzle as they might over the meaning of the volcanic rocks of Clougher Head or the curious fossils at Ferriter's Cove, they could not have discovered the rifting and crashing of continents. The impressive bulk of their data, painstakingly amassed and mapped at a scale of six inches to the mile, was not enough to unravel the riddle of the rocks. Their data were a prelude only. A century would pass before the real geological symphony began.

Near the same spot at Ferriter's Cove where Jukes, Du Noyer, Griffith, and Murchison conferred on the meaning of the Dingle Beds, I pick up a pebble of yellow mudstone. The stone contains the intaglio impression of a bivalve shell, a brachiopod from the late Silurian. It is four hundred million years old. The fossil brachiopod is remarkably similar to living shells that I might find today on a nearby beach. It is an object lesson in the endurance and resilience of life. It is a token of that which endures in the face of change.

The fauna recorded in the rocks of Ferriter's Cove— the brachiopods, bryozoa, corals, gastropods, and trilobites—lived in a shallow-water environment on a storm-lashed continental margin. (This we can deduce from the nature and disposition of the fossils.) At that time Ireland was in two parts. The northern half of Ireland was a coastal province of North America—a fragment of Greenland, actually—and the southern half was part of Europe. Separating the two halves of Silurian Ireland was the narrow remnant of an ocean called Iapetus by geologists. The continents of North America and Europe had been moving toward each other for two hundred million years, since the Cambrian period, and the floor of the ocean that separated them was being squeezed out of existence, pushed down below the continents ("subducted"), into the red-hot mantle of the Earth. As the ocean floor was squeezed into the mantle it generated heat. Above the subducting sea floor the crust melted, and liquid rock forced its way to the surface, erupting in chains of volcanoes along both continental margins. It was at this time that the volcanic rocks at Clougher Head had their origin. In Silurian times, life had not yet made the transition from sea to land; as the two halves of Ireland converged, the marine creatures that lived on the shores of Europe and North America were about to be caught in the big crunch.

I turn the yellow pebble—my lucky charm—in my hand, with its impression of a creature that lived in that other world, and I wonder what Jukes, Du Noyers, Griffith, and Murchison made of the creatures in the rock. The mid–nineteenth century was a time of intense debate about the meaning of fossils. It was the prevailing opinion among the general populace that the world was no older than 6,000 years, that it had been created as described in the Book of Genesis, and that whatever was observed in the record of the rocks must in some way be made consonant with Scriptures. A common view held that fossils were remains of animals and plants overcome by the flood associated with Noah. But another opinion was growing in the minds of the geologists who tramped the wild places in tweeds and frockcoats to reconstruct the "annals of a former world" (the phrase is that of the Scottish geological pioneer James Hutton). Most British geologists were attracted to the ideas of the Frenchman Georges Cuvier, put forward in his *Recherches sur les ossemens fossiles de quadrupedes.* Cuvier supposed that the Earth had been overwhelmed on several occasions in its history by "catastrophes," the most recent of which was the deluge that Noah survived. These catastrophes brought about the extinction of many forms of life, allowing only enough species to escape in order to repopulate the Earth. Fossiliferous strata in the sedimentary succession were the residue of these episodes of violence—the product of flood, earthquake, or volcanic eruption.

Cuvier's radical ideas stirred up considerable popular interest, and fossil hunting became all the rage. In 1814, the young son of a cabinet-maker found a sea monster of spectacular proportions—an ichthyosaurus—in the cliffs at Lyme Regis on the Devon shore. Another child of that same cabinet-maker, Mary Anning, discovered in 1821 the first nearly complete skeleton of a plesiosaur. At almost the same time, the surgeon Gideon Mantell found in Sussex the fossilized bones of a remarkable beast that he called Iguanodon. By 1842 it had become apparent that these monsters from the past belonged to a tribe of extinct reptilian creatures unlike any that exist today. Richard Owen christened them Dinosauria, or "terrible lizards." These monsters could have had no place on the Ark. These discoveries and the controversy they excited must have been on the minds of

Jukes and his friends in 1856 when they hammered trilobites out of the rocks at Ferriter's Cove and surveyed the volcanic formations at Clougher Head. Like their geological contemporaries, they were laying the groundwork for a new Creation. A few years later, Darwin would confound the world with a dramatic retelling of the Earth's past. It was a story that did not require the interventions of a willful God.

There must have been a single decisive moment when it was possible to say, "The gods are dead." Perhaps it was when Mary Anning uncovered the skeleton of Plesiosaurus in the Liassic cliffs near Lyme Regis. Anning was not a member of that confraternity of geologists who were engaged in technical debates about the sequence and meaning of Cambrian, Ordovician, Silurian, and Devonian strata. She did not have a part in those ongoing squabbles between catastrophists and uniformitarians, or between Neptunists and Vulcanists, or between the followers of Murchison and Sedgwick on the one hand and those of De la Beche on the other. She was not concerned with "truth" or with reputation. She was a young girl who took pleasure in rock and sea and discovery. She sold her plesiosaurus to the Duke of Buckingham for the considerable sum of £200, and she used the money to support her widowed mother. Her story made great press. The monster in the rock captured the public's fancy.

The geologists of Jukes's generation struggled to find a way to make the story of the fossils compatible with the story of the Scriptures. But it was too late for that. A huge gulf of geologic time had opened between them and their Creator, a gulf too broad to see across and too deep to ford. The god of Genesis had become irrelevant. There was a new story of Genesis now to be written, and each chapter of that new book embraced a hundred million years. Today, at Ferriter's Cove, I stand on a shingle of stones that are 350 million years old. I roll my lucky stone between my fingers. I weigh it out in the palm of my hand. I trace the flutes of the embossed Silurian brachiopod with the ball of my thumb. If there is an incarnation, then this is it. If there is a resurrection, this brachiopod has found it. If we are made in the image and likeness of God, then *this* is his image.

Sometime about 350 million years ago, the southern half of Ireland joined with the northern half. The floor of the intervening sea, and its population of Silurian fauna, was crumpled between. Rocks were thrust high into the air. The strata were fractured. Brachiopods, gastropods, corals, and trilobites were folded into the hearts of mountains. Greenland and Europe met, and Ireland was united. But the story was not finished. The newly unified continent split along a new line not far to the west and drew apart, with a new ocean filling the rift (the present Atlantic). The mountains along the old suture were eroded away. A second mountain-building impulse from the south pushed up new mountains (Brandon Mountain, at my back, was the product of that new thrust, called the Hercynian). Erosion stripped away most of the newer mountains, and at last the fossils in the heart of the mountains were exposed to glisten in the sun on the shingle at Ferriter's cove. "A thousand years in your sight are as yesterday," sings the Psalmist. A million years here at the cove—or ten million, or a hundred million—are as yesterday. Before the mountains were begotten and the world was brought forth, from everlasting to everlasting, the sea has clamored on this shingle. Stones have been broken from the hearts of mountains. Monsters have been set free.

"You make an end to them in their sleep," says the Psalmist; "the next morning they are like the changing grass, which at dawn springs up anew, but by evening wilts and fades....Seventy is the sum of our years, or eighty if we are strong. And most of them are fruitless toil, for they pass quickly and we drift away." Joseph Beete Jukes died in Ireland. He never ceased to consider Ireland the land of his exile and his place of trial. During his twenty years as director of the Irish Geological Survey, 117 sheets of the one-inch geological map of Ireland were published, as well as fifty-five sheet memoirs that he edited. More than 1,000 six-inch field sheets were compiled during his tenure. It was a monumental achievement that remains even to this day the foundation of all Irish geological studies. Jukes died in a private lunatic asylum in the Dublin suburb of Glasnevin. His wife removed his body to Warwickshire, where his grave has since been lost.

For the past several days I have read and re-read the journals that record the anguish and the hopes of my father's last days. They seem to have a message for me if only I can read it. One of the journals records a dream. My father dreamed that he was a ball of twine, rolling down a spiral staircase and unwinding. As he bounced from step to step he passed his children going up. They were puzzled, he notes in his journal, as they watched the ball of twine bounce by. My father was all his life a teacher, and the journals were his last lesson. In the final days of his life, his hope became focused on three things, in almost equal measures—God, medical science, and his own observations and theories. He was "covering all the bets," and he was not the first dying man to do so. But neither God, nor medicine, nor his own precisely contrived graphs and theories saved him. In the end, the ball of twine ran out. In the end, there was only a fray of thread.

The odds, of course, were against him. He was an amateur caught in the gulf between God and science, those two great excluding poles of his life. He was an amateur, and day by day the professionals came to visit, the priests and the doctors, with their firm grip on what is important. He tried to convince them he had found something new that also mattered. And they humored him, as professionals generally humor amateurs. What he did not know, or chose not to believe in the helplessness of his pain, was that the day had passed when an amateur could bend God's ear or determine the course of science. The God who cured the leper, raised Lazarus, and comforted Lawrence on his bed of flame was gone from this world of pain and glory. And science, too, was equally beyond my father's reach. He was an amateur, like Mary Anning, digging fossils from the bedrock of his pain, and there was no Duke of Buckingham to reward his efforts. Still, at the end, he discovered a "unit of energy," that special kind of energy that for him was the essence of health, the thing that covered pain like a mantle of soft snow and now was melting away. He discovered a precise geometrical "unit," and his "cycles" took on a quantified character. Now his graphs climbed and fell by measured degree, and he caught a vision of a way to build degree upon degree so that the cycles would acquire a secular trend, upward, toward recovery. He tried to convey this information to the doctors and the priests, and they humored him, sympathetically, as professionals must, for they knew that now even cobalt radiation and chemotherapy were no longer useful, that the cancer had spread to every cell of his marrow, that his wasted body was now just a sackful of alien cells with a life of their own, and that whatever secular trend might be relevant to the course of his life was downward, inevitably, toward extinction.

The last battle of my father's life was fought on the only field that was left to him, the field of sight, taste, touch, smell, and sound. He collected and recorded the data of the senses with the zeal of a scientist. What he made of these things did not save him, but for twelve terrible weeks it gave him a purpose and a hope. His journals constitute the testament of a man who never lost faith in the world of the senses, even as it slipped away. He knew that there was an order to his personal chaos, and on that point the priests and doctors agreed. It was in making himself a part of that order that he found whatever immortality was to be his destiny.

VESPERS

The Gift of Luminosity

IT HAS BECOME SOMETHING of a ritual. Every clear evening for a month I have climbed the mountain behind the house to look for the green flash. I have sat on the high rocky spine of the Dingle Peninsula and watched the sun sag into the North Atlantic. Tonight the air is particularly stable and clear. The view to the northwest is unobstructed to the far horizon. There are no clouds, except for a few cirrus wisps above the mountains across Dingle Bay to the south. At this latitude in the summer the sun does not "set"; rather, it "glides," west to north along the horizon, slowly losing altitude, until at last it seems to be rolling upon the surface of the sea and only inadvertently sinking. My pursuit is venerable. For twenty years I have looked for the green flash, although only casually—catch as catch can—taking advantage of a clear sunset horizon whenever the opportunity presented itself, always unsuccessfully. Now I have determined to make a more serious effort to see the flash. Each day I have watched the weather and minded the time of sunset.

And on promising evenings I have climbed the mountain, sat down with my back to the stone wall that bounds my neighbor's high pasture, and waited.

The green flash is a momentary burst of color that can be seen just at the top edge of the sun as it disappears below the horizon at sunset, or as it appears above the horizon at dawn. I became aware of the existence of the green flash in 1965, when I read an article on the subject by the astronomer D.J.K. O'Connell of the Vatican Observatory. The effect described by O'Connell was so evanescent, so unexpected, so marvelous, that I have pursued it ever since. All my life I have been a collector of nature's rarest and most subtle gifts—nature's *cryptophenomena.* I am not talking about Loch Ness monsters, or pots of gold at the end of rainbows, or other purported creatures or objects that if they were real would be of a spectacular nature. Rather, I am talking about aspects of the *ordinary* and *presently real* that hide in their very delicacy— very young moons, certain ephemeral kinds of frost, and the zodiacal light are examples—things that require for their observation nothing but knowledge and patience. The attraction of the green flash as described by O'Connell was irresistible. But the green flash turned out to be grandly evasive; twenty years later, I am still waiting and watching.

Scientific interest in the green flash had its origin with a work of science fiction. Jules Verne's *Le Rayon Vert,* published in 1882, described a search for the mysterious ray and excited the curiosity of naturalists. Until O'Connell's research it was widely assumed that the green flash was a subjective phenomenon or an optical illusion. Retinal fatigue was commonly held to be the "cause" of the flash. After looking into a brightly colored light our eyes become fatigued, and upon looking away we see the complementary color; so, according to this theory, after looking for a while at the setting sun, which is red, we see the complementary color, green, when the sun disappears below the horizon or when we briefly avert our vision. The "blaze" of color, then, is not in the sun, but in the eye. O'Connell's research proved the subjective theories false. Here, for the first time, were color photographs of the flash. The photographs were not easy to make. The band of color to be captured on film is exceedingly narrow and fleeting. To obtain their success, O'Connell and his colleagues were required to overcome formidable problems of optics and exposure. But the evidence of the photographs is indisputable. The green flash is not an artifact of the eye. At the top margin of the sun's disk—in photograph after photograph—is a brilliant strip of emerald green!

And so here I sit, letting nature tease and tantalize, waiting for a gift of light to be thrown my way. A blink of the eye will be enough to miss it. I have, over the course of the past month, invested more than a dozen hours in the search for a ray of light that persists for a fraction of a minute. It is not the sort of activity that will make me rich; it is a sublime sort of foolishness. But I am a creature of signs. The flash, if obtained, will be like a signal from *out there* in the sea of mystery, a signature of the Absolute, a spectral revelation. And meanwhile, there is no place I could more pleasurably spend my time than here, with the hidden Absolute all around me in the air and sea, in the purple mountains, in the sheep that move languidly in the fields below, in the natural garden of wildflowers that generously softens the wall at my back; waiting, expectantly, with a universe holding its breath, to be stained—for an instant—green by a curious quirk of light and air.

◐

I have seen my share of lights in the sky. I have seen the aurora borealis and the zodiacal light. I have seen sun dogs and rings around the moon. I have seen double and even triple rainbows. I have seen the midnight sun. But I have not seen the green flash.

On several occasions I have seen what might be called ULOs—"unidentified luminous objects." Once, returning late at night from a hiking trip in the White Mountains of New England, I saw streamers and star-bursts of color shimmering on the dark sky. What I saw might have been the aurora borealis, except that the lights were low in the *southern* sky—not a likely place to see the aurora. I was convinced that I had seen something of a unique and extraordinary origin, perhaps a localized shower of powerful cosmic rays that had caused the atmosphere to fluoresce. Later, I learned that the display of light was an artificial aurora produced by NASA by injecting a cloud of barium into the upper atmosphere with an experimental rocket launched from the Naval Observatory Station at Wallops Island, Virginia.

Anyone who minds the sky and is reasonably obser-vant will sooner or later see ULOs. I have seen inexplica-ble patches of luminous cloud in parts of the sky far away from the sun. (Could it have been sunlight reflected from a large body of water?) Once I watched what I took to be a satellite moving across the night sky. In every respect the object had the proper characteristics of a satellite. It moved on a typical polar orbit and at the proper apparent altitude and speed. The light from the object varied periodically, as reflected sunlight often varies from a satellite that tumbles or rotates as it moves. Then, quite suddenly, the "satellite" reversed direction, something no real satellite could possibly do. I am convinced that what I saw was not an airplane; I classify the object as a ULO. Not long ago, as I walked home in darkness from the pub in Ventry, I saw a light dancing in the dark hollow of the glacial corrie near the top of Mount Eagle. The light moved too quickly to be a lantern in someone's hand. It seemed to dart back and forth between the walls of the corrie, sometimes dipping toward the waters of the lake, sometimes soaring toward the top of the headwall cliffs. The image of that active light is still vivid in my memory, but the source of the light remains a mystery. Unless...

The Irish naturalist Robert Lloyd Praeger, in his autobiographical book *The Way That I Went*, describes the case of "luminous owls." According to Praeger, a Miss Mildred Dobbs was the first to report these curious "birds," after they had been brought to her attention by the ferryman at the Villierstown crossing of the Blackwater River in County Wexford. On several occasions Miss Dobbs and her sisters watched mysterious lights that they took to be birds. They saw the lights swoop and dive along a distant hillside. The lights moved irregularly, sometimes disappearing, sometimes becoming nearly stationary, and then, moving rapidly, crossing the river where no light carried by a human hand could possibly go; the lights were reflected in the still water of the river. Other local people confirmed the observations. Were the lights actually birds? A report in the *Times* of London in 1907 described soaring lights that had been seen on a number of evenings in Norfolk. A local gamekeeper declared that he had shot one of the moving lights and found it to be an aged and half-starved barn owl. A Shropshire correspondent to the *Times* added that he had known a pair of barn owls with this "gift of luminosity" (Praeger's words), but only when the birds were in poor condition. Is it possible, then, that owls, in certain circumstances, are self-luminous? And, if so, is the source of the light within the birds themselves, or is it a luminescent algae that grows on the feathers of weakened birds? Praeger left the matter open, and as far as I know the story of the luminous owls has been carried no further by naturalists. Could the moving light that I saw in the corrie on Mount Eagle have been the flight of a bird with the "gift of luminosity"? Barn owls are known to hunt far and wide, but a weakened bird would not likely be so high on the mountain. And it is difficult to imagine that a bird could emit enough light to be mistaken for a lantern at a distance of more than a mile. The light I saw on Mount Eagle is best left in the category of ULO.

The gift of luminosity! There is apparently nothing to which it cannot be given. Owls in the Blackwater Valley glimmer on the wing. I have seen stones that shine with their own light. I have watched the sea break in eddies of phosphorescence. It is said that the earth emits light during earthquakes. Red flashes have been observed on the moon. Certain toadstools radiate sufficient light to be seen from far off. These are gifts given, a grace of lights. And now I wait for my own elusive gift of light, *le rayon vert*, the green flash, a sunset trick of air and space, that long-sought scintillation, that spectral spectre, that willfully radiant will-o'-the-wisp.

I once published a short essay on my search for the green flash, and I heard from several readers who had seen the flash from places as diverse as Cape Cod and Peru. One correspondent sent a photograph. I have two friends who often saw the green flash from the deck of a tanker plying equatorial waters. The green flash exists. It is not a trick of the retina.

My efforts to see the green flash have not been confined to the west coast of Ireland. I have watched for the flash from the western coast of the United States, from the Outback of Australia, and from an island in the South Pacific. And I have watched from the eastern coast of the United States at sunrise (admittedly, a more difficult way to observe the flash, which precedes the sun into the sky and requires an exact foreknowledge of the time and place of sunrise). The flash can be seen only if the horizon is sharp and distant and free from haze, conditions best found on coasts, in high mountains, or in deserts. O'Connell notes that Egypt offers exceptionally favorable circumstances for observing the flash, and he points out that there is some evidence that the ancient Egyptians were familiar with the phenomenon. According to O'Connell, there is an Egyptian stone pillar dating from 2000 B.C. that shows the rising sun colored blue above and green below. The Egyptians seem to have believed that the sun is green during its nocturnal passage beneath the Earth—a lovely idea that may have derived from observations of the green flash at both sunset and sunrise.

The cause of the flash has now been carefully established. As the sun sets (or as it rises), its light strikes the Earth's atmosphere at an oblique angle and passes through a great thickness of atmosphere. The atmosphere reduces the velocity of the light and the light rays bend (refract), in the same way that a stick appears bent when it is partly submerged obliquely in water. The degree of bending depends upon the wavelength or color of the light; violet rays are deflected most, red rays least. As with a prism, this differential bending spreads the colored rays into a rainbow (dispersion). When the sun sets, its colors should disappear over the horizon one by one—red first, violet last—depending upon the degree of bending. But the orange and yellow rays are absorbed by water vapor, oxygen, and ozone in the atmosphere. The blue and violet rays are scattered away from the path of the light by molecules of air. The color least affected by its passage through the atmosphere is green, and that is what—briefly—the observer sees. In producing the green flash, nature uses almost every gimmick in its optical bag of tricks: refraction, dispersion, absorption, scattering. It is a dazzling production, a bit of technical wizardry, a marvel of optical legerdemain.

"There is a kind of poetry, even a kind of truth, in the simple fact," writes the naturalist Edward Abbey. I sit on a hill in the west of Ireland and wait for a *fact*. I am not waiting for the heat, the sweetness, and the music that were heaven-sent to Richard Rolle, or for that self-luminosity that is said to have bathed certain mystics in the moment of trance. It is a light I seek, and to see it will be as sweet as honey; but the light will be *out there,* and it will issue from the sun. I am waiting for the simple *fact* of the green flash.

The most valued facts arrive unexpectedly, and nakedly unadorned. That is what happened one day last autumn as I wandered in the forests of a wild aster, exploring the Amazonian luxuriance of the last of the season's flowering plants. With the plant splayed on the stage of a dissecting microscope and my eyes affixed to the oculars, I plunged among stamens and pistils, shouldered aside sepals and bracts, and waded in pools of golden nectar. It was not a scientific exercise but a simple excursion of the senses, a wallowing in color, texture, bristle, sheen, excess, riches—a wallowing in simple fact.

It turned out that I was not alone that day in the leafy forest of the aster. Suddenly, up and out of the honey-caked style of a flower, over the stigma, stretching across space to an anther, down a filament, along a flower ray, came stepping some great creature as out of the prehistoric past. Now the beast advanced toward me; now he backed away. I whirled the focusing knob of my instrument to follow his progress. At this magnification the creature filled the eyepiece—a six-legged dinosaur, a steel-plated stegosaurus, a rainbow-hued triceratops— glistening in his iridescent armor, swinging his great bony head from side to side, lifting his legs one by one to make his ponderous way up and down the pathways of the aster.

At last the monster stopped to plunge his long proboscis into the stem of the plant. As he fed, I had a chance to make notes of his distinguishing characteristics, and, in particular, of the two remarkable horny prongs that protruded from the wingcovers. This insect was new to me, but the facts of his description were sufficiently unusual to promise an easy identification when I got to my handbooks. Or so I thought.

A basic identification was not difficult. It did not take me long to ascertain that the dinosaur on the aster was a member of the family of insects called snout beetles. But among the many illustrations in my handbooks, and in other, more detailed treatises that I found in the library, this particular snout beetle was not to be found. And no wonder. The beetles are a spectacularly diverse order of insects. They constitute two-fifths of all the insects on Earth. And the snout beetles are the most varied of all the clans of beetles. Snout beetles exist in more variations than any other member of the animal kingdom. There are more than 50,000 species that have been described worldwide, and more than 2,500 in North America alone. The chance that I would find this particular beast in a standard handbook was slim indeed. Practically all of the snout beetles are plant feeders. Many of them are serious pests of cultivated plants. They chew holes in fruits, nuts, stems, leaves; they are eclectic in their tastes, voracious in their appetites. My snout beetle was typical—as I watched, he filled his gut with the juicy substance of the aster.

There are probably tens of thousands of species of snout beetles waiting to be discovered. For all I knew, the creature I watched last autumn was being observed for the first time, a species unknown to science, making its debut on the stage of my microscope. It would take a better entomologist than I to know the truth, to place this insect in a proper scheme of things, to add his declension to the corpus of science: Phylum Arthropoda, Class Insecta, Order Coleoptera, Family Curculionidae, Species... shall I say... asterosaurus. The fact of the snout beetle, the simple unadorned fact, would have to be enough. If I had my choice, I would rather *know*, to say the insect's name, to describe exactly its habits and habitat, to enter, insofar as I can, into the particular patterns of its life. But in lieu of that, the *fact* will do, the surface of the thing, the vivid prong-horned proboscidian presence in the eyepiece of my microscope.

Then shall I be, like Edward Abbey, "pleased enough with surfaces"? There are underlying patterns in nature—taxonomies, classifications, orders of relation, genealogies, laws. There are days when I am content to contemplate these patterns, as described by science on the printed page, as one might read in silence the score of a Bach fugue, marveling at the carefully woven threads of counterpoint that provide the underlying structure of the music. And there are other days when the music is enough, in the ear alone, unanalyzed, resonant, imperative, all-enclosing—days like the one when I watched the thunder-footed snout beetle forage in the glistening jungle of a wild aster, or days like this one when I wait for an elusive emerald aberration of light—and I am content with the shimmering reality of surfaces, stark immediate facts, a poetry of here, the truth of now. Facts! "What else is there?" asks Abbey. "What else do we need?"

◐

Robert Lloyd Praeger, who related the story of the

luminous owls, tells of another, stranger creature that shines by its own light, the Carrabuncle of County Kerry. The Carrabuncle is first mentioned in Charles Smith's *Ancient and Present State of the County of Kerry*, published in 1756, as having been seen in the Lakes of Killarney. Smith quite naturally supposed that the name referred to the familiar precious stone rather than to an animal. The confusion was resolved in 1883, when Henry Hart, climbing on Brandon Mountain on the Dingle Peninsula, encountered a man who told him of a creature called the Carrabuncle that lived in Lough Veagh, where people gathered freshwater mussels for the pearls they contained. "These come off an enormous animal," Hart was told by his informant, "which is often seen glistening like silver in the water at night. The animal has gold and jewels and precious stones hanging to it, and shells galore; the inside of the shells shines with gold." Five years later, the naturalist Nathaniel Coglan, also on Brandon Mountain, heard more of the Carrabuncle. This time the fabulous beast was resident in Lough Geal ("the shining lake"). It appears, he was told, only once in seven years, and then it lights up the whole lake. If only you could catch the Carrabuncle, Coglan was assured, your life would be blessed with riches.

I have climbed on Brandon Mountain every year for twice seven years, and I have looked into each of its dark lakes, but I have not seen the Carrabuncle. Nor do I expect that I will. The Carrabuncle of the Kerry lakes is no more real than the monster of Loch Ness. Anthropologists and etymologists might usefully pursue the Carrabuncle to discover its folkloric origins or how it came about its curious name, but zoologists will properly stick to certifiable fauna, of which there are several

species hereabouts hardly less fabulous than the Carrabuncle. There is, for example, the Natterjack Toad, an
amphibian from the region of the Mediterranean that
can be found in Ireland only in the sand banks about
Castlemaine Harbour at the eastern end of Dingle Bay.
This golden-colored warty little frog (paradoxically called
locally "the black frog") emerges from its burrow only at
night and runs rather than hops across the sand in an
unfroglike fashion. How it came to Castlemaine Harbour
from so far away is not known; if by ship, then once it
burrowed into Kerry sand it lost all further interest in
travel. Another southerner that found its way to Kerry is
the Greater Spotted Slug, a fine character as slugs go,
shiny black with silvery yellow spots. This particular
species of slug is found nowhere else outside of Portugal
and Spain. The Greater Spotted Slug has the curious
talent of being able to elongate itself so that it takes on
the appearance of a worm, and it can thereby insinuate
itself into the smallest crevice. Conchologists have reported putting the fat slug into collecting boxes with
loosely fitting lids, only to find that their precious
specimen subsequently made good its escape by transforming itself into a string and slipping free. I have not
encountered the Natterjack Toad, but I have come across

the Greater Spotted Slug. It is a creature as pleasant to look upon as any Carrabuncle, and hardly less difficult to find. The Greater Spotted Slug moves with a patient langour, and one wonders about the details of its migration from so far to the south. Did it come creeping millimeter by millimeter up over the Pyrenees, across France's central massif, along the plains of Normandy, to a channel port, there to wait for passage to Rosslare or Cork? Almost certainly not. The mysterious Kerry slug very likely came to Ireland by ship, directly from Portugal or Spain, and it is another confirmation of the ancient communication (based mostly on smuggling) that existed between Dingle and the Iberian Peninsula.

Like Scotland's Loch Ness Monster, the Carrabuncle of the Kerry lakes is the sort of creature that might find among the credulous a million advocates. Properly exploited by the local tourist office, the Carrabuncle could attract a huge influx of visitors to the peninsula, possibly for a Carrabuncle Festival to be held once every seven years. There is within the human condition a compelling appetite for the fabulous, typically sated with monsters, mermaids, chimeras, hippogriffs, and an imaginative assortment of gods. Meanwhile, the real wonders are all about us, burrowing into sand and slipping ribbonlike into cracks, wonders hardly less marvelous than any unicorn. And there is no need to wait seven years for their appearance. It is true that the Greater Spotted Slug emerges only in wet weather, but we have enough of that in Kerry.

◗

Christ appeared to Julian of Norwich and showed her a little thing the size of a hazelnut that he placed in the palm of her hand. It was, she tells us, "as round as any ball." She looked at it and wondered what it might be. Christ answered her: "It is all that is made."

It is all that is made. The Earth is a sphere that I can hold in the palm of my hand, glistening in its damp seas, misted with air. It is wound up like a ball of twine from a single thread that encompasses everything that exists. Luminous owls move at night on a thread of light. The Greater Spotted Slug slides on a thread of slime. It is the same thread. In his *Travels on the Amazon and Rio Negro,* Alfred Russell Wallace makes mention of the Carbunculo, a mystical animal of the Upper Amazon and Peru: Is there an etymological thread of connection between the South American Carbunculo and the Carrabuncle of Kerry? Does the thread stretch from the Amazon Basin to the slopes of Brandon Mountain, with a knot somewhere near Portugal or Spain? I go about looking for toads and slugs and tales of creatures that shine with gold and pearls; they are bits of the thread that binds up the world. I hold the planet in my hand like a ball of twine; if I unwind it, the thread will stretch from one side of Creation to the other.

I wish it had been I who found the Snake of Milecross. Milecross is a village in Ireland's County Down. A snake was discovered there in 1831. But wait! Everyone knows there are no snakes in Ireland. Snakes were banished from Ireland by Saint Patrick in the fifth century—or so the story goes. The person who found the snake at Milecross first imagined it to be an eel. The creature was taken to Dr. J.L. Drummond, the noted Irish naturalist, who pronounced it to be a bonafide reptile. The idea of a "rale living sarpint" having been found within so short a distance of Saint Patrick's burial place created a sensation among the country people. One clergyman preached a sermon in which the snake was cited as a portent of the coming Millenium. Others supposed that the snake foreshadowed a great epidemic. Old prophecies were dredged up, and not a few people were convinced that the end of the world was at hand.

It turned out that the unfortunate reptile was one of a half-dozen harmless English garden snakes that had been purchased in Covent Garden Market in London by a Mr. James Chambers, a gentleman of County Down, who wished to ascertain if it was the climate or the soil of Ireland that was naturally inimical to snakes. He turned the snakes loose into his garden at Rath-gael, three miles from Milecross, and they promptly escaped into the countryside. Four of the snakes were eventually captured and killed, including the one that excited such consternation. The other two snakes never turned up, and it is not known if they were subsequently the victims of Patrick's curse or an inclement quality of the climate or soil.

The belief that Saint Patrick banished snakes from Ireland persists even today. But Ireland was without snakes long before the arrival of Patrick. Solinus, writing in the third century, describes Ireland as a place noted for

its lack of reptiles. The Venerable Bede, in the eighth century, takes note of the absence of reptiles on Irish soil—and makes no mention of Patrick. He tells us that when snakes are transported to Ireland on ships, they invariably expire when the ship reaches the midpoint of the Irish Sea, presumably exterminated by their first whiff of pure Irish air. (The story was apparently not communicated to the snakes purchased by Mr. Chambers in Covent Garden.) Bede says that people in Britain suffering from the bite of vipers can be cured by drinking water in which the scrapings of Irish books have been steeped.

So snakes were absent from Ireland long before Patrick. But if Saint Patrick did not drive the snakes out of Ireland, then who did? Or *what* did? The answer is both topological and climatological. During the most recent ice age the flora and fauna of the British Isles were pushed south by advancing glaciers. For a hundred thousand years, most of Britain and Ireland lay under a mantle of ice. Then, about 10,000 years ago, when the ice caps on the northern continents began to retreat, the plants and animals came creeping back, first to Britain, and then to Ireland. For a time, while quantities of sea water were still piled upon the continents as ice, Britain and Ireland were connected to the rest of Europe by dry land. Across these natural bridges the creatures moved. As the ice melted further, the level of the seas rose and the lowest-lying parts of the European continent were flooded. Britain and Ireland became islands. The snake, deliberate creature that it is, made its way successfully from France to Britain while the present channel was still dry. But its migration farther west was cut short by the rising waters of the Irish Sea. Saint Patrick did not drive the snakes out of Ireland; the ice drove them out—if they were ever here at all—and the sea kept them out. But it has been 10,000 years since the end of the ice age, and it is surprising that in all that time snakes have not somehow managed to reestablish themselves in Ireland—in the same way as the Natterjack Toad or the Greater Spotted Slug—by stealing a ride in the hold of a ship, nested in a cargo of produce or grain. Perhaps descendents of the uncaptured Milecross snakes are still about, lying low, knowing in some instinctive way of the fate that waits them if they show themselves in violation of Patrick's supposed malediction. Let an English garden snake poke its head out from under an Irish rock and I'll keep my mouth shut, for the sake of the snake. But I will take note. It would be another wrap of a wound-up world—slugs and toads, Carbunculos and Carrabuncles, the advance and retreat of glaciers, the rise and fall of the sea—a world as composed and complete as a ball of twine, as compact as a hazelnut held in the palm of a hand.

At last, the disk of the sun touches the horizon, and the sea is briefly tangent to the star. The conjunction of the sun's disk and the horizon creates a powerful illusion of largeness. The sun seems to swell to twice its ordinary

diameter. I hold out my hand at arm's length, and—yes—the disk of the sun is still only half as wide as the width of my little finger, exactly the same as when the sun is high in the sky. And now, as the disk begins to slip below the horizon, all sorts of things begin to happen. The circle elongates and wavers like a banner. Then, just as the sun is about to disappear from sight, bubbles of color break free from the disk and rise—one, two, three—to quickly dissipate in quavering air. It is the moment for the green flash. I watch the place of the setting sun, afraid to blink. There are shimmerings of orange and pink, but no green. And then it is over.

Once more I have been disappointed. Again the flash has failed me. But I am not displeased. Some things should remain elusive. "What makes the desert beautiful," said Antoine de Saint-Exupéry's Little Prince to his pilot, "is that somewhere it hides a well." The green flash is my hidden well.

COMPLINE

The Knowing That Unknows

IRELAND SITS WELL UP ON THE SHOULDER of the globe. In these latitudes in midsummer the sun sets late. There is still a hint of twilight in the northern sky when our publican in Ventry blinks the lights in the pub, the signal that it is half past eleven o'clock and time for ordering last pints. I have had enough drink. In the amber glow of Irish ale and good conversation I strike off up the bothareen toward home.

By the time I reach the high road and emerge from the dark hedgerows of bramble and fuchsia, the stars are appearing one by one. It is a Van Gogh sort of sky, splashed with gaudy swirls and streamers of starlight. Not long ago a scholar analyzed Van Gogh's paintings of the night sky and found that they were more "realistic" than anyone had supposed; apparently it is possible to recognize in the paintings the patterns of certain constellations. Perhaps. But Van Gogh saw something in the night sky that is not to be found on any star map I have seen. He saw the stars as vortices of color, and not as white dots. Van Gogh's stars are huge multi-hued cyclones that pull us up by the hair and empty us out of the Earth like water from a broken vessel, as are the stars that shine above me tonight. Look, *now*, at Antares, low above Valentia Island, exploding like a Roman candle, outlandishly red. Or there, above Mount Eagle, golden Arcturus, waving like an oriflamme. Or near the zenith, scintillant Vega, like a smoke hole in the tent of the sky, aswirl with blue and silver light. I go all giddy. It is no wonder Van Gogh went mad. A glance at a sky like this one is enough to unhinge any reason. Once these stars have spilled their color onto night's black canvas, there's no putting it back. We are splotched and splattered with it and go blubbering about, wildly shaking our heads, like madmen or village idiots.

I sit on a grassy bank at the side of the "road of the fairies" to wait and watch. Smoky Vega smolders at the zenith. The star's name is derived from the Arabic *Al Nasr al Waki*, "the swooping eagle." And, indeed, Vega appears to swoop, to plummet luminously, exactly as Van Gogh painted it. It dives toward me, straight down from the roof of the sky. It is twenty-seven light-years away, 160 trillion miles, but I swear that if I reached out my arm I could touch it. What the Arabs did not know is that the name they gave the star is more than poetry, more than metaphor. Vega *does* dive toward us, in a literal sense; or rather we dive toward Vega. The star is very near to that place in the sky called the solar apex. It is the place among the constellations toward which the sun's motion among the stars of the galaxy is carrying us. The sun is flying toward Vega, and we go with it. We are falling toward Vega at twelve miles per second, spiraling down onto that blue star out of the black backdrop of the universe. We will be there in half a million years.

Up the smoke hole, down the drain! The stars are more than we bargained for. They are thermonuclear furnaces, incandescent with the heat of vanished matter, globes a million miles in diameter, or ten million, or a hundred million, voluptuous presences. Give Van Gogh this—he saw the stars for what they are, undisguised by distance. Some people say that Van Gogh's stars, those vertiginous volcanoes of color, were a product of his madness. Perhaps it was the other way around.

This is the world I love best—the world lit by starlight. There are a few dozen electric lights burning in the parish below me, and I can make out another dozen or so lights on the Iveragh Peninsula across Dingle Bay, including the resolute beacon of the Valentia Harbour lighthouse. My immediate environment—the grassy bank, the hedge of honeysuckle and fuchsia, the wild irises and foxgloves massed in the ditch—is illuminated solely by the light of stars. Vega, at the zenith, is a thousand times less bright than the full moon, fifty million times less bright than the sun. But multiply Vega's faint light by the 10,000 stars of the summer Milky Way, and it is illumination enough.

In the bardic schools of ancient Ireland, the young poets-in-training, having been set in the evening a theme for composition, retired each one to his private cell, a cell furnished with nothing more than a bed and perhaps a peg on which to hang a cloak, and—most importantly— without windows, there to compose the requisite rhymes, taking care to observe the designated rules as to syllables, quartans, concord, correspondence, termination, and union, in *total darkness*, throughout the remainder of the night and all the next day, undistracted by the least ray of the sun, until the following evening at an appointed time when a light was brought in and the poem written down. An eighteenth-century account of the bardic schools by the Marquis of Claricarde asserts that the discipline of darkness was imposed so that the young poets might avoid the "Distractions which Light and the variety of Objects represented thereby commonly occasions," and in darkness "more fully focus the Faculties of the Soul" upon the subject at hand. From the Marquis' language one might suppose that the soul has a light of its own, that it glows with a self-luminosity, like the owls of the Blackwater Valley, and that the soul's crepuscular light is drowned out by the light of day. Certainly poets, like mystics, have traditionally been creatures of the night. The world of daylight is a world of impenetrable surfaces, resplendent, metallic, adamantine. In starlight, surfaces are transparent, like the flesh of a hand held to a bright light, and the soul sees into objects and beyond. But there is a danger in starlight—the danger of infinite dilution. There is a danger that the soul will leak away like water into loose soil, or be dispersed like breath in wind. Could that be why the poets of the bardic schools shut themselves up in *total* darkness to compose their verses, without the light of a single star? The light of one star is enough to prick night's dark skin, and the enclosing sphere of the sky goes pop like a balloon, and we fall out of ourselves, upward, toward Vega, at twelve miles per second, into Infinity.

Vega is a typical main-sequence star, a star in the full vigor of its life. Its surface temperature is roughly twice that of our sun. Vega is three times larger than the sun and three times more massive, and the amount of energy that streams from Vega's surface is sixty times greater than the energy that flows from our own star. If there were an Earthlike planet near Vega, at an Earthlike distance, it would be seared in that star's prodigious heat. But Vega very likely does not have planets—not yet, at any rate. The IRAS orbiting infrared telescope detected around Vega a Saturnlike ring of glowing dust. The ring is probably a planetary system in the early stages of formation. If this is so, then Vega is a new star, only "recently" condensed from cosmic dust. And stars like Vega do not live long in any case, by comparison with a smaller star like our sun. Vega will burn itself out in only a billion years. By the time Vega's planets have settled into place and become amenable to the appearance of life, Vega will have exhausted its nuclear fuel and entered its violent decline.

At Ireland's latitude Vega dominates the summer night, by virtue of its brilliance and its commanding position near the apex of the sky. The light of the star does not make its way to my eye as a directed ray, as it might be easy to suppose. The energy produced in Vega's thermonuclear core moves away from the surface of the star in every direction, out past the glowing ring of protoplanetary dust, into the great emptiness of interstellar space, becoming as it expands always more dilute. You can think of the energy that leaves Vega at a particular instant as being carried away from that star on the surface of an imaginary sphere. The radius of the sphere increases at 186,000 miles per second, the speed of light, distending the star's light over an ever-increasing area, stretching the energy density of the light always thinner. At our distance from Vega—twenty-seven light-years—the star's light is dispersed over a spherical surface with an area of 320 septillion square miles (an unimaginably large number—320 followed by twenty-eight zeros). When we see Vega, it is with the infinitesimally small fraction of Vega's light that just happens to be intercepted by the pupils of our eyes. How can I suggest how little of Vega's light our eyes actually gather up? Compare the area of the pupils of our eyes (twice the area of this letter *O*) with the area of the surface of a sphere with a radius of twenty-seven light-years. Or here is another analogy: If the light radiated by Vega at a particular instant is compared with all of the sand on all of the beaches of the world, then the fraction of the light that will eventually enter my eye is a single grain. No, the analogy is not yet mathematically correct. Let the light radiated by Vega be compared with the *entire material bulk* of the planet Earth; then the fraction of the energy that will enter my eye is still far less than a grain of sand. It is out of that pinch of starlight that I construct the star.

I can work all of this out on paper, and still it seems a miracle. I lie back on this grassy bank and the light of *10,000* stars enters my eyes in sufficient quantity to enable my brain to form images of the stars. Ten thousand subtle but distinct wavelets of energy enter my eyes at slightly different angles from out of the depths of space, and by some miracle my eyes and brain sort it all out, put each star in its proper place, recognize the familiar patterns of the constellations, construct a Milky Way, and open my soul to a universe whose length and breadth exceed my wildest imagining. Starlight falls upon me like a gentle rain. It blows across me like a furious wind. I am soaked and shaken.

And there is more. Out of the minuscule quantities of starlight that reach the Earth, astronomers, with the proper instrumentation, can deduce the sizes, distances, densities, and compositions of the stars. The astronomers take those grains of starlight and with a grating or a prism spread them out into spectra and recognize in the patterns of color (or the absence of color) the telltale radiations of the very same elements out of which the Earth is made—hydrogen, oxygen, calcium, iron, and so on. Vega's substance is the same substance as the iris in the ditch! It is an astonishing revelation of the relatedness of everything that exists. The stellar spectra of the astronomers are another wrap of a wound-up universe, a universe as compact as a hazelnut in the palm of my hand.

Julian of Norwich asked: *What is the use of praying if God does not answer?* In starlight, God answers. Starlight blows through my body like wind through the hedge. My atoms ebb and flow in a cosmic tide of radiation. Vega surges into luminescence and electrons do handsprings in the cortex of my brain. Planets are gathered in Vega's dusty brim; I am warmed by their gentle heat. If you sip the sea but once, said the Zen master, you will know the taste of all of the oceans of the world. Tonight I have sipped 10,000 stars. I have tasted the universe.

◑

My fingers close spontaneously about a small smooth stone. Even in starlight I can see that it is a limestone pebble from the road. Here on the Dingle

Peninsula we live on Devonian and Silurian sandstone, but ten years ago, when the County Council improved our road, they trucked in gravel from the Vale of Tralee, thirty miles distant, crushed limestone, a part of the heavy mantle of limestone that once lay upon all of central and southern Ireland and covers most of it still. Those beds of gray rock extend from one side of Ireland to the other. They are thousands of feet thick; in some parts of Leitrim and Sligo they are almost a mile thick. The limestone consists of the skeletal remains of organisms such as algae, bryozoa, corals, and mollusks that have the ability to extract calcium carbonate from seawater. When the organisms died they were deposited on the floor of an ancient sea and turned to stone. No other sediments, such as riverborne sand or silt, were carried into the sea; the substance of the pebble in my hand is entirely the work of living creatures, mostly microscopic animals that built calcite bodies in the form of globes, stars, helices, pinwheels, spikes—dazzling architectures that I have often examined on the stage of a microscope. The limestone rocks of Ireland are graveyards that were piled high for tens of millions of years with life's refuse. When I walk along this road, I tread upon the bodies of my ancestors, single-celled organisms that perfected the ingenious chemistries of photosynthesis, respiration, sexual reproduction, and the building of shell and bone—creatures as intimately a part of my past as my own parents, however far removed from me by innumerable branchings of our family tree.

Like those other bits of stone I saw fall from the sky on the night of the Perseid meteor shower, the pebble in my hand is heavy with the dust of stars. The atoms of calcium and oxygen and carbon here clustered into molecules of calcite ($CaCO_3$) were fused in the cores of stars. Take forty hydrogen nuclei—forty protons from the first instant of Creation—and squeeze them in the core of a massive star until the temperature soars to tens or hundreds of millions of degrees; the protons fuse, some of them shedding their positive charge to become neutrons (and in the process throwing off those elusive particles called neutrinos; the neutrinos fly out from the core of the star, their penetrating power is unmatched, they are not at all impeded by the star's bulk; the star floods the universe with cast-off neutrinos). At some stage in the star's life, the protons and neutrons cling to form the nucleus of a calcium atom with forty nuclear particles— twenty protons and twenty neutrons. When the star dies catastrophically, the calcium atoms (and other elements, including carbon and oxygen) are blown into space, to become eventually the substance of new stars and planets. In our own sun there are 700 oxygen atoms, 400 carbon atoms, and two calcium atoms for every million atoms of hydrogen; these heavier atoms were created in stars antecedent to our sun, stars that illuminated the younger galaxy with a brilliant blue light. One hundred septillion (10^{26}) hydrogen nuclei were processed in the interiors of Vega-like stars to create the pebble in my hand. And, in fusing, a thousandth part of the mass of the hydrogen was converted into pure energy and radiated as starlight. The galaxy scintillated in the execution of this exquisite work. And it goes on still. As Vega burns, it thickens, becoming heavy with the elements of life. This carbonate pebble in the palm of my hand is the ash of starlight. A galaxy glittered to contrive its bulk.

One hundred years ago the eminent physicist Lord Kelvin confidently asserted that the work of science was complete. Newton's mechanics and Maxwell's theory of electromagnetism had been wonderfully successful in explaining a wide range of physical phenomena. There was nothing more to learn, said Kelvin, *in principle.* Only "two small clouds" remained on the horizon to trouble him. One was the anomalous behavior of short-wavelength radiation from an incandescent light source (blackbody radiation), and the other was the unexpected negative result of the Michelson-Morley experiment on the propagation of light through the aether.

By the end of the nineteenth century the two small clouds had grown into thunderheads. The first bit of trouble was finally resolved by Planck's theory of the quantum; the second was resolved with Einstein's theory of relativity. Quantum physics and relativity are cornerstones for our present understanding of the world. The two nettlesome phenomena, so perceptively cited by Kelvin, were like rabbit holes that led into Wonderlands of fresh understanding.

If we are sensible, we will be cautioned by Lord Kelvin's premature closure on nature's ability to surprise us. Science has been impressively successful, but every accumulation of knowledge, like the earthen bank on which I sit, is full of rabbit holes. Enter a rabbit hole—into quantum physics, say, or relativity—and that Wonderland has its own rabbit holes leading to yet other exotic terrains. ("Goodness," said Alice. "Things flow about so here.") One doesn't have to be a Lord Kelvin or a Planck or an Einstein to find a rabbit hole to enter. A pebble can serve—if I chose to enter it. A leaf of grass will provide ingress to Infinity. The ancients believed that the stars were pinholes in the dome of the sky, through which shone the light of an outer, more wonderful world. And it is true: Every star is a rabbit hole into another world. In the course of a lifetime of starry nights I could not explore them all.

The constellation Lyra is astride the summer Milky Way. I have often explored the constellation with binoculars (I have also used telescopes, but for light-drenched summer nights I prefer binoculars). It is a region of shimmering delights, in the midst of summer's thickest stream of stars, a warren of rabbit holes, an alphabet of entrances. *Alpha Lyra*—Vega, "the swooping eagle," the fifth-brightest of all the stars; there are 200 stars closer to us than Vega and not one of them, including our own sun, is half so luminous; Vega glistens in an aureole of protoplanets. *Beta Lyra*—Sheliak, "the tortoise," possibly the most intensely studied star in the sky, replete with paradoxes; you cannot see them separately, not even with a telescope, but Sheliak is actually two stars in close orbit about each other; the two members of the Sheliak system are closer to each other than Mercury and our sun, and they revolve about their common center of mass every twelve days; the stars periodically eclipse each other's light, causing the apparent star to vary in brightness; streams of luminous gas surge back and forth between the intermingled atmospheres of the two com-

ponents of Sheliak, so that first one star is the most massive and then the other. *Gamma Lyra*—Beta's almost twin at the bottom of the Lyre, but steady as a rock; I have used Gamma to gauge the variations of the light of unsteady Beta. *Delta Lyra*—a widely separated binary system easily resolved with binoculars; one star is red, the other blue, a ruby and a sapphire set in a cluster of tiny diamonds. *Epsilon Lyra*—near Vega, the famous "double-double"; Epsilon is a single star to the unaided eye, a striking double in binoculars, and a telescope resolves each star of the double into a pair, so that the system actually consists of four huge suns, each perhaps shepherding a flock of planets, locked in a dance of circles within circles within circles.

Pick a rabbit hole at random—say, the northern component of Epsilon 1, one of the four stars of the "double-double"—and plunge down it. Emerge into a world as intricate as our own, a planet in orbit near a white star. The planet has two suns in its sky; one sun is a thousand times less bright than the other, but bright enough so that there is no night for half a year. It is a world strangely different from our own (there are monsters that gleam in the depths of lakes with the radiances of gold and pearls), and yet same (frozen water falls with six-cornered symmetry). And in the sky of this planet of Epsilon 1, Vega also shines—during the dark nights that come at intervals of a year—but less brightly than on Earth; it is a star of the fourth magnitude only, and rather unspectacular. And a fraction of a degree away from Vega in the sky of this planet there is a solitary yellow star of steady light, a star that is visible only with powerful binoculars. It is our sun.

With binoculars on a clear night I can count a

thousand stars in the constellation Lyra, a thousand pinpricks in the dome of night, a thousand rabbit holes leading to Infinity. I tumble down them. I fall head over heels into a universe of inexhaustible mystery. I fall out of *this* body and *this* Earth into a universe in which galaxies fly like wind-blown seeds from the first fierce impetus of the Big Bang.

And now comes the time to face the ultimate questions, as one must always face them on nights such as this one when starlight soaks the ground like a summer rain, staining the stony brown soil the darker color of wet peat and moistening the limestone pebbles of the road a deeper gray. The irises in the ditch stand on tiptoes to catch their share of starlight—and of the neutrinos falling from Vega that zip through their splayed yellow fingers, plash into the ground, and go on to China. How do I ask the questions without sounding the fool? I am not a philosopher. I am not a theologian. I will ask the questions exactly as I learned them as a child. Let them stand erect like the irises, foolishly flapping their clichés, venerable in their fool's silks: *Who am I? Why am I here?*

The starry night is not a time for conscious profundity. The questions come unbidden. They come like threadbare Magi to the place of incarnation (incarnate: "make flesh"; *He came and dwelt amongst us*). Incarnation can happen anywhere, anytime, I suppose, so why not here on this hillside, tonight, fleshing out this hedge, fattening these stones, pulping up my own skin and bones? *Who am I?* Philosophy is of no help, unless like a spider I want to weave a web of my own substance. Science is not of much use either; rather, science considerably complicates the question, blurs the boundaries of self (like a wide aperture lens that sharpens the image on a single plane but loses depth of field) and makes this hugely intricate "I" go out of focus. Where are the boundaries of the self? Is that the end of me, down there, at the tips of my toes? Does the "I" stop there? Do the soles of my feet enclose a philosophical entity? Like the pebble in my hand, this lump of Carboniferous plankton, I am stardust—galactic cobwebs here temporarily concreted into an entity of uncertain dimension. My matter intermingles with earth and air. I suck in stardust with every breath. Atoms of starstuff leak out of my body through the pores of my skin. Is the "I" then only an eddy in a stream, a cyclonic cluster of atoms in a stardust sea, an impermanent turbulence, a contrail of air? What kind of a self is that?

Perhaps the "I" is not the substance, but the form— the helix of the whirlpool, the logarithmic curl of the turbulent eddy—like one of those gorgeous "organic" curves that are generated with the mathematics of fractals. Am I the snowflake's hexagon stamped upon the storm? Am I the galactic spiral inscribed upon stars?

Surely the self is more than substance, more than

form. The "I" must surely be the *conscious* thing, the reluctant philosopher, the makeshift theologian. Let me shake that conscious "self" out like a basket of laundry; what do I find? Astonishing! Here is the cardboard game of "Chutes and Ladders" that I played at the age of four (my earliest memory). And here are the cupboards on my grandmother's porch that are filled with dark medicinal jars of pickles and jams (and here is that other terrifying jar on the shelf in the high school biology lab). Here, tumbling from the basket, are the verses of poems I memorized at the age of ten. And the guilts and raptures of adolescence. Here are novels I read in college. And the residue theorem of the theory of complex variables (miraculous! beautiful!). The trajectory of Comet Swift-Tuttle. Devonian deltas and Carboniferous seas. The spectrum of Vega. And more. Much more. Where did it all come from? How did it all fit into so small a basket? In certain experiments on the physiology of memory, flatworms of the species *planaria* were taught to move toward light to find their food; then the trained worms were ground up and fed to untrained worms, which—fattened on the substance of their unwitting mentors—exhibited an ability to move toward light without being trained. Is memory, then, molecules? Could I ingest the differential calculus for breakfast? Is there a knot of tissue somewhere—*in here*—the size of a hazelnut, that has impressed upon it "Chutes and Ladders," *The Magic Mountain*, Comet Swift-Tuttle...to be called up precisely at will, or higgledy-piggledy in dreams? Is that tangled knot of molecules the "I"?

It hardly makes sense to think on it. The self swims in intricacy. Whatever the "I" is, it is as small as a hazlenut and as large as the universe. When Christ appeared to Julian of Norwich and handed her the small round thing, red blood poured down from the wounds on his brow. *The Word was made flesh.* Flesh and blood, hedge and irises, earth, water, starlight. *Who am I?* I am who am. *Why am I here?* The devil only knows. I will leave the questions for the theologians and live without the consolations of philosophy. I will sit on this starlit bank and shiver in my ignorance, red blood pouring through my veins, a wind of atoms blowing in and out through my nostrils and the pores of my skin, pummeled with particles from the cores of stars, Vega-drenched, sandstone-lifted, terrified, unconsoled, undefined, ecstatic.

●

On the night of July 16, 1850, Vega became the first star to be photographed. For one hundred seconds Vega posed at the sky's zenith, while astronomers at the Harvard Observatory used the slowly turning fifteen-inch refractor to fix an image of the star on a plate of glass coated with a silver chloride emulsion. That daguerreotype presumably still exists, in a file drawer at the Cambridge observatory, sparkling in its diffraction spikes, a tangible part of the collective memory of humankind.

Out of the laundry basket of collective memories I now pull verses—verses that follow questions unbidden—verses distilled like the photographic image of a star from the dark night. The verses are those of a sixteenth-century Carmelite friar, born Juan de Yepes in the village of Old Castile but known to us by the name he took upon profession of his vows—John of the Cross. John was involved in the movement for reform of the Carmelite order that had been initiated by Teresa of Avila. With Teresa, he advocated a return to simplicity, contemplation, and prayer in the life of the brothers and sisters. Feelings about reform ran deeply within the order, and passion soon erupted into violent hostility. In 1577, John was kidnapped by members of the unreformed brethren and carried off to the Priory at Toledo. There, until his dramatic escape eight months later, he was held in a dark, foul-smelling closet, half starved and often beaten by his captors. In total darkness, without pen or pencil to write them down, he composed the stanzas that now come to mind. John's poetry affectionately extols the beauty of the created world—"wings flickering here and there,/ lion and gamboling antler, shy gazelle,/ peak, precipice, and shore,/ flame, air, and flooding well." He records what he calls the "knowledge of the evening"—as opposed to the daylight knowledge that will come (according to John) only when the soul meets the Creator face to face—a knowledge that enraptures even as it taunts us with God's absence.

The knowledge of the evening. It is all I have, and all I ask for. Where is the hand that opened to let fly the galaxies? Absconded. Where is the eye that fixed Vega at the zenith? Gone. John of the Cross asks, "Where have you hidden away,/ lover, and left me grieving, care on care?/...imploring the empty air." The Lover is hidden; that is the terrible reality of our fate. I cannot pray; I can only praise. There is "no sign for me to mark,/ no other light, no guide/ except for my heart—the fire, the fire inside."

But the air is *not* empty. It streams with starlight. From the cores of stars neutrinos fall out of the night. The darkness between the stars—and here between bank and hedge—is full, like the inside of a cooling oven, with the invisible warmth of the Big Bang. The air is full. The hedge swells with intricacy. The stones teem. "Lavishing left and right/ a world of wonders, he went streaming by/ the woodland, quick as light." Luminous owls trace ribbons of light in the dark corrie. The setting sun stains the mountains green. Every interstice of creation glows. The fire, the fire inside! There is no darkness; all things become visible in the light.

John of the Cross, by means of ropes twisted from pieces of blanket and tunic, let himself down from his wretched cell into the darkness. Across the night city he made his way to a Reformed Carmelite convent, "looking like an image of death," and was given pears stewed in cinnamon. The following spring he was at a mountain hermitage in Andalusia, at a place gifted by nature's unbitter hand. There he completed his verses: "Earth ending, I went free,/ left all my care behind/ among the lilies falling and out of mind."

Whatever John of the Cross saw or felt of God's daylight face cannot be mine. We are separated, he and I, by centuries and by science. John of the Cross lived in a world that was 6,000 years old and bounded *just up there* by the dome of night; my universe is measured by geological eons and reaches to the quasars. John's Earth was the still nexus of Creation; mine is flung like a droplet of spray from a sea of galaxies. John believed himself created in God's image; I am an atom on a flung drop. But still, across the intervening centuries, John speaks to *this* dark night; his verses stand free of religious allegory, free of theological commentary; they are great free-standing arches of praise: "O dark night my guide!/ night dearer than anything all your dawns dis-

cover!/ O night drawing side to side/ the loved and lover."
Vega beckons from the zenith. My soul leaks away.
Among the irises, Earth ending, I fall out of mind.

●

 Somewhere out there in John's dark night—a night
both tender and frightening—a comet is coming nearer,
scattering streaks of anticipation across the summer sky.
Tonight I have counted half a dozen shooting stars, a
respectable number for any time of the year, but only a
fraction of what August will bring when the Earth
intersects the orbit of Comet Swift-Tuttle. One of the
meteors I saw tonight was possibly a Perseid; it had the
proper radiant—in the constellation Perseus, over the
northeastern horizon—and as it zipped south it neatly
parted the Milky Way, grazed Vega, and bisected the Lyre.
Was it a crumb of Comet Swift-Tuttle? I collect it
greedily. I add it to my skimpy hoard of revelations—a
crumb of comet, a moving light in a mountain corrie, the
clap of a heron's wing, a pebble picked up from a hill road
that tastes of limey seas—talismans, insignias, ciphers,
signs, tossed up from a sea of mystery: "Though some
would wade, the wave's unforded still./ Nowhere a bottom, measure as you will/ in dark of night."

 Nowhere a bottom! I have studied science. For
thirty years I have explored every recess of what science
has learned about the world we inhabit, probed every
corner of natural philosophy, gone down every rabbit
hole. There is no bottom. Every apparent bottom is false.
Down, down I have gone until the bottomlessness itself
has become a thing, a tangible sponge of limitless interstices that soaks up soul and self. "Whom should I
adore," asked Lawrence, "the Creator or the creation?"

And the night answers: *The creation!* Beautiful. Terrifying. Infinite. Deep. In the transparent air of the summer night there is a taste of salt from the sea: It is the taste of God. I press a limestone pebble against my lips: It is the kiss of his mouth.

Once I climbed Brandon Mountain with a friend. It was a fine bright day as we set out from the bridge at Brandon Creek. By the time we had ascended a thousand feet, clouds had rolled in from the sea. At 2,000 feet we entered an unbroken cover of cloud. At the saddle between Brandon and Masatiompan we cautiously hesitated, turned south, and moved carefully along the ridge toward the summit, mindful of the steep cliffs that fell away sharply to the east. And then an amazing thing happened! As we approached the summit of the mountain, our heads popped out of the clouds; for a moment our decapitated heads rested on white cotton like laboratory specimens. Another step—shoulders emerged. Then torsos. Step by step we lifted our bodies out of white fleece into a sky of stunning clarity and perfect blue. The summit of Brandon Mountain was an island of rock that protruded ten feet above the cloud, a hundred square feet of solidity in a universe of air. From horizon to horizon the top of the cloud stretched as smooth and uninterrupted as the surface of the sea. White cottony cloud! It seemed as if we could have stepped off our island onto it. It seemed as if we could have walked across it to those other islands to the south, the distant summits of McGillicudy's Reeks. A temperature inversion of remarkable definition had reduced our world to a clean slate, a featureless interface of blue and white, a *tabula rasa*, a fresh creation. A borrowed metaphor came to mind: *Knowledge is an island surrounded by a sea of mystery.* On Brandon's cloud-truncated summit, that metaphor was made startlingly real.

Tonight, the scrubbed simplicity of that day on Brandon Mountain is gone. The bank, hedge, and ditch are full, scribbled over with complexity, as dense with discriminations as any cabala. A Milky Way of axioms, theorems, and corollaries drapes the sky like a bountiful sash. *Description is revelation. Seeing is praise.* The heavens declare the glory: I will praise with the tongues of angels. The firmament showeth forth: I will sound the lyre. At home on my desk there is a photograph of the star Vega invested with its halo of circumferential radiant dust. It is not a visual image; it is a computer color-coded representation of infrared data. A photograph of Vega made with ordinary light would show a solitary star, as on that first star photograph made more than a century ago, an unadorned point of light, a luminous circle shrunk by distance to a central point. But Vega radiates more than visible light. It glows warmly in the long-wavelength radiation of the infrared. If you possessed infinite sensitivity, you could put out your hand and feel Vega's heat on your palm. No, you could not; the Earth's atmosphere absorbs the star's feeble infrared rays. But telescopes in orbit above the Earth's atmosphere, equipped with sensors that are tuned to the wavelengths of the infrared, can "feel" the heat of the stars, and they have shown Vega glowing like an ember. And more! Around Vega there is a brim of dust, half a light-year wide and as warm as toast. Comet dust. The dust of meteors. Grains of nickle and iron. Silicates. Ices. Dust that entrains volatile gases and water vapor. Enough dust to make a dozen planets, planets with seas and atmospheres. But not planets yet. The dust is still dispersed into a flat disk, but slowly it is yielding to the clumping tendency of gravity—the halo is condensing into grains, the grains into nuggets, the nuggets into asteroids, the asteroids into worlds—worlds as numerous as flakes of snow condensing out of a storm, as same and as different.

A grainy stuttering of heat on a simulated photograph—knowledge condensing from a sea of mystery, extending the shore along which we might encounter *God.* (Can that ancient, much-abused word still have currency in an age of science? Perhaps not. But let it stand, like a distant horizon, like a foreign shore.) *Este saber no sabiendo,* "this knowing that unknows," is what John of the Cross called it, the knowing that takes place *just here* on the surface of the eye where Vega and the thought of Vega are one. Photons of radiant energy stream across the light-years, wind-whipped whitecaps of visible light and the longer swells of the infrared, to fall upon the Earth out of the dark night—denying, revealing, hiding, making plain. I am soaked by starlight; I am blown by a stellar wind. I am bent low in that downpour of revelation.

◑

INDEX